Free at La

DATE DUE

Free at Last?

Free at Last?

U.S. Policy Toward Africa and the End of the Cold War

Michael Clough

COUNCIL ON FOREIGN RELATIONS PRESS

NEW YORK

COUNCIL ON FOREIGN RELATIONS BOOKS

The Council on Foreign Relations, Inc., is a nonprofit and nonpartisan organization devoted to promoting improved understanding of international affairs through the free exchange of ideas. The Council does not take any position on questions of foreign policy and has no affiliation with, and receives no funding from, the United States government.

From time to time, books and monographs written by members of the Council's research staff or visiting fellows, or commissioned by the Council, or written by an independent author with critical review contributed by a Council study or working group are published with the designation "Council on Foreign Relations Book." Any book or monograph bearing that designation is, in the judgment of the Committee on Studies of the Council's Board of Directors, a responsible treatment of a significant international topic worthy of presentation to the public. All statements of fact and expressions of opinion contained in Council books are, however, the sole responsibility of the author.

If you would like more information on Council publications, please write the Council on Foreign Relations, 58 East 68th Street, New York, NY 10021, or call the Publications Office at (212) 734-0400.

Library of Congress Cataloguing-in-Publication Data

Clough, Michael.
    Free at last? : U.S. policy toward Africa and the end of the Cold War / by Michael Clough.
    p.   cm.
    Includes bibliographical references and index.
    ISBN 0-87609-104-4 : $14.95
    1. Africa, Sub-Saharan—Foreign Relations—United States. 2. United States—Foreign Relations—Africa, Sub-Saharan. 3. Africa, Sub-Saharan—Foreign Relations—1960– 4. Cold War.
I. Title

DT38.7.C57   1992   91-43338
327.73067—dc20   CIP

92 93 94 95 96 97   PB   10   9   8   7   6   5   4   3   2   1
Cover Design: Whit Vye

For Helen Kitchen and Carl G. Rosberg, and to the memory of Franklin H. Williams

CONTENTS

Acknowledgments   ix

1. Introduction   1

2. Geopolitics and Africa   5

3. U.S. Economic Interests in Africa   14

4. African Images and African Realities   20

5. U.S. Domestic Constituencies   26

6. Changing American Realities   40

7. Changing International Realities   54

8. The Limits of U.S. Economic Power in Africa   63

9. The Global Reach of American Society   68

10. A Dismal Balance Sheet   76

11. Models of Success   101

12. Strengthening Civil Society in Africa   110

13. A New U.S. Policy Toward Africa   117

   Notes   125
   Index   136

ACKNOWLEDGMENTS

This book is best understood as an essay based on over a decade of studying U.S. policy toward Africa from various angles. During those years I have benefitted from the experience and wisdom of a list of people far too long to include here completely. For me, as for literally hundreds of others in the field, Helen Kitchen has been a constant source of support. David Doerge, Charlayne Hunter-Gault, Martin Lowenkopf, John Marcum, Robert Price, Carl Rosberg, and M. Crawford Young have also each provided vital support at crucial moments.

The seeds of the idea for this book were planted in the summer of 1989 by a request from the Rockefeller Foundation that I organize a small project on how to elevate Africa's place on the U.S. foreign policy agenda. Those seeds sprouted and grew because of the assistance and encouragement of a number of key people. My associates in the African studies program at the Council on Foreign Relations were indispensable. Without the efforts of Michelle Bassin, who coordinated the early stages of the project, and Nomsa Daniels, this book would not have been written. Mary Jane Fox and Russell Pechman also provided critical assistance. My greatest editorial debt is to the Council's Director of Studies, Nicholas X. Rizopoulos. I am also indebted to Peter Tarnoff, the President of the Council, and David Kellogg, Director of Publications, for their support and encouragement. As with most Studies efforts, Judith Gustafson played an indispensable administrative role in this project. Two people were responsible for shepherding this book through the publication process: Suzanne Hooper and Judy Train. David Haproff was there at the end when we needed him most.

I would also like to acknowledge those who made this book possible by making that part of my world that has nothing to do with Africa work. Amy, Ryan, and Daniel have sustained me both through the writing of this book and, more importantly, through all the experiences that went into getting to the point in my life where I could write it. In addition, I want to thank the guys in the mailroom—Phil, Tony, Ian, Hector, Santos, and Walter. Without them and the fantasy baseball league, this book might have been finished a lot faster, but my life would have been a lot duller. Last but not least, I must give credit to Arcuri's Pizza and Deli which provided the coffee that jump-started my brain each morning.

1

INTRODUCTION

For nearly four decades, U.S. policy toward Africa* was shackled by the Cold War. From the end of World War II until late 1984, Washington's interest in the continent fluctuated with changing estimates of the threat posed by real or imagined Soviet gains. Consequently, American policymakers defined their options narrowly; they seldom gave priority to initiatives that did not serve U.S. strategic interests. Private groups seeking to influence our Africa policy were forced to rationalize their recommendations in geopolitical terms. Those that could not do so (or refused even to try) were ignored. The result was a policy fundamentally at odds with the expressed commitment of the United States to democracy and development. U.S. officials overlooked and often excused repression, injustice, corruption, and economic mismanagement in such African countries as Kenya, Somalia, Sudan, and Zaire that were willing to oppose Moscow. They repeatedly opposed popular nationalist movements in southern Africa that they perceived to be on the wrong side of the great East-West ideological divide. And they often turned a blind eye to human suffering in countries that seemed to them to have no strategic value.

In the fall of 1984, the chains that bound U.S. policy toward Africa (and the rest of the world) started to loosen. Although few analysts recognized it at the time, a process was set in motion that

* Throughout this book, "Africa" generally refers to sub-Saharan or black Africa. There are two reasons for limiting the scope of the study in this way. First, the U.S. foreign policy community tends to treat North Africa (Algeria, Egypt, Libya, Morocco, and Tunisia) more as part of the Middle East than as part of Africa. Since 1969 the Department of State's Bureau of Near Eastern Affairs has exercised primary responsibility for North African countries. Second, many of the points made in this book do not apply as much to North Africa as they do to sub-Saharan Africa. For example, U.S. interests in the Mahgreb countries are both different from and more substantial than U.S. interests in the sub-Saharan countries. In addition, American constituencies concerned with Africa tend to focus more on the south than they do on the north. But the division between north and south, especially as it concerns countries such as Chad and the Sudan that straddle the regional divide, is far from absolute.

1

led to the end of the Cold War. On September 23, President Ronald Reagan met with a senior Soviet official (Foreign Minister Andrei Gromyko) for the first time since taking office. The two adversaries agreed to reopen discussions on arms control and other global issues. Over the next few months, the Soviet government, headed by an aged and ailing Konstantin Chernenko, signaled its interest in a new and less confrontational relationship with the West. In mid-December, Chernenko's then little-known deputy, Mikhail Gorbachev, visited Great Britain and declared that the Soviet Union "will not be the one to start a new round in the arms race."[1] Out of these tentative beginnings came a revolution in international politics, a revolution that has fundamentally transformed American foreign policy priorities.

With the end of the Cold War, the United States is free at last to develop a new relationship with Africa.[2] But there is a serious danger that this opportunity will be squandered. One reason is that the Bush administration has failed to provide any leadership on African issues. Neither the president nor any of his senior foreign policy advisers has displayed any real interest in the continent. Instead, they have delegated responsibility for policy toward Africa to midlevel officials with limited vision and no domestic political base. These officials operate with considerable latitude so long as they heed three injunctions: "Don't spend much money." "Don't take stands that might create domestic controversies." "Don't let African issues complicate policy toward other, more important, parts of the world." But the failure of the Bush administration to craft a new policy is more a symptom than a cause of the problems that have afflicted U.S. relations with Africa.

Despite the president's incantations about "a new world order," neither he nor the foreign policy Establishment* more generally has a clear vision of the U.S. role in the post–Cold War international system. Absent such a vision, it is difficult for them

* The foreign policy Establishment consists of a small but growing group of individuals who move in and out of senior positions in government and play leading roles in shaping the foreign policy debate. It also includes academics, journalists, lawyers, and other professionals with experience and expertise in international relations. While the Establishment of the 1990s differs significantly from the Establishment of the 1940s and 1950s, it is still very much a force in the making of U.S. foreign policy.

to convince themselves—or others—that there is a need for U.S. involvement in distant parts of the Third World, such as Africa. The fact that the United States has few concrete, material interests on the continent reinforces doubts about the need for a substantial American presence there. Moreover, Africa's diverse, sometimes chaotic, and often depressing realities make it difficult for many Americans to relate to the continent. Finally, the absence of powerful, cohesive, and enduring domestic constituencies generally concerned about African problems has reduced the pressure on Washington to develop an effective policy.

U.S. policy toward Africa is now at a crossroads. Washington can head in any of three directions. It can continue to lurch back and forth from issue to issue, professing deep concern about the continent's plight and criticizing Africans for their past failures, while doing precious little to back up words with deeds or resources. Alternatively, it can declare, openly and honestly, that U.S. interests in Africa are so marginal and the ability of the United States to play a useful role so limited that it is pulling back in order to let others who are more interested and able take the lead on the continent. Or it can attempt to develop realistic policies that will encourage sustained American involvement in Africa. This book is an argument for option three.

The United States needs a policy toward Africa that can enlist Americans in an effort to foster and sustain African civil society* and by so doing help to promote democracy and devel-

* "Civil society" is an old theoretical concept that has recently gained new currency. It has been defined in a variety of ways. According to Phillippe Schmitter of Stanford University, civil society consists of "intermediary organizations and arrangements that lie between the primary units of society—individuals, families, clans, ethnic groups of various kinds, village units—and the ruling collective institutions and agencies of the society" (quoted in Commission on Behavioral and Social Sciences and Education, National Research Council, *Democracy: Proceedings of a Workshop* [Washington D.C.: National Academy Press, 1991], p. 16). It constitutes, in the words of Czechoslovakia's President Václav Havel, "the independent life of society" (Havel, et al., *The Power of the Powerless*, Armonk, N.Y.: M.E. Sharpe, 1985, p. 65). In Africa, as Michael Bratton has written, civil society consists of "a rich array of forms: from modest, informal, local-level mutual aid associations to registered, nonprofit NGOs with well-funded development programs; from syncretic religious movements which mobilize followers with fundamentalist and apocalyptic messages, to interest groups of producers and professionals which seek legal recognition and access to the public policy process" ("Enabling the Voluntary Sector in Africa: The Policy Context," in *African Governance in the 1990s: Objectives, Resources, and Constraints*, Working Papers from the Second Annual Seminar of the African Governance Program, The Carter Center of Emory University, Atlanta, Georgia, March 23–25, 1990).

opment throughout the continent. Precedents for such a policy were provided in the mid-1980s by the American response to famine in Ethiopia and the continuance of apartheid in South Africa. As Chapter 11 illustrates, in both cases a surge of public concern forced Washington to change official policy and inspired many private citizens and organizations to take independent action. The result was a mix of public and private actions that saved the lives of many Ethiopians, helped to force the South African government to begin negotiations to end apartheid, and enriched civil society in both countries. Today the principal objective of U.S. Africa policy should be to encourage similar responses to challenges in other parts of the continent.

To succeed, a new U.S. policy must be based on a hardheaded assessment of American interests and African realities. It must take into account both the strengths and weaknesses of the U.S. foreign policymaking process. It must be consistent with the changing position of the United States in the international system. And, most important, it must be grounded in an understanding of the past failures of U.S. policy in Africa.

Hopes for a grand U.S. initiative in Africa similar to the Marshall Plan are certain to be disappointed. The domestic constituency that would be needed to win support for an ambitious rescue operation does not exist; and even if it did, the United States currently lacks the economic resources and global clout to carry out such a plan. Similarly, strategies that depend primarily for their success on the ability of the White House and State Department to set priorities, marshal resources, and implement new policies are likely to fail. Senior officials in the executive branch will always have too many other preoccupations, or too little interest in the continent, for them to take the lead on African issues. What is needed instead are firm legislative guidelines to ensure that U.S. officials do not repeat the mistakes of the past, combined with positive measures to encourage and capitalize on the growing interest of a diverse range of private American groups in a variety of issues affecting the continent.

2

GEOPOLITICS AND AFRICA

Throughout the Cold War, geopolitical considerations determined Africa's place on the U.S. foreign policy agenda. Interest in the continent ebbed and flowed with shifts in perceptions of the potential impact of African events on the global interests of the United States. With the end of the Cold War, it is no longer easy to predict how much attention U.S. officials will pay to African developments.

Geopolitics first began to influence U.S. policy toward Africa in the decade following World War II. During the late 1940s and 1950s, the Truman and Eisenhower administrations were concerned primarily with ensuring that Western Europe became a stable bulwark against Soviet expansion. This preoccupation caused them to abandon the traditional role of the United States as an outspoken critic of colonial rule. U.S. policy toward Africa was greatly affected as a result.[1] American officials worried that criticism of colonial policies might weaken or alienate allies in Lisbon, London, and Paris. For example, in 1953 Henry Byroade, the deputy assistant secretary of state in charge of African affairs, remarked: "Let us be frank in recognizing our stake in the strength and stability of certain European nations which exercise influence in the dependent areas. . . . We cannot blindly disregard their side of the colonial question without injury to our own security."[2]

Mason Sears, who served as U.S. representative to the United Nations (UN) Trusteeship Council throughout the 1950s, put it more bluntly: "Because of the Cold War, [Secretary of State Dulles] decided to subordinate the promotion of African freedom to what he considered the overriding necessity to support our NATO allies and their colonial policies."[3] Fear that the abrupt decolonization of Africa might lead to political disorder and create opportunities for Communist penetration reinforced Washington's conservative tilt. "It is a hard, inescapable fact,"

Byroade declared, "that premature independence can be retrogressive and dangerous."[4] Because of these concerns, the Eisenhower administration chose not to play a strong role in the decolonization debates of the 1950s.

In the late 1950s, a reassessment of Africa's geopolitical significance began. The independence of Tunisia, Morocco, and Sudan (1956), and Ghana (1957); Guinea's abrupt break with France (1958); and the Algerian revolution (1954–62) signaled the beginning of the end of the African colonial era. The collapse of over a half century of European hegemony on the continent occurred just as the Soviet Union under Nikita Khrushchev's energetic leadership was searching for opportunities to expand its influence in the Third World. In 1955 Western officials learned that the Soviet Union had agreed to supply President Gamal Abdel Nasser of Egypt with arms via Czechoslovakia. This conjuncture of events turned Africa into an open field for superpower competition. In a report to President Dwight Eisenhower following a visit to Africa in 1957, the first by a senior American official since the end of World War II, Vice President Richard Nixon predicted that "the course of [Africa's] development . . . could well prove to be the decisive factor in the conflict between the forces of freedom and international communism."[5] To meet this challenge, Nixon recommended the creation of a separate bureau of African affairs in the State Department. With the establishment of such a bureau in 1958 and the commissioning of a series of National Security Council (NSC) policy reviews, the United States began to organize itself to compete with the Soviet Union for the political loyalty of Africa's newly emerging states.

American interest in Africa peaked during the Kennedy era. Although cloaked in the rhetoric of liberal internationalism (and reinforced by a genuine desire to help fledgling African states), John Kennedy's eagerness to become involved in the continent's affairs was driven by the same geopolitical concerns voiced by Nixon, his rival in the 1960 presidential election.[6] This was evident in the language used by Arthur Schlesinger, Jr., who served on the Kennedy White House staff, to describe the administration's early appraisal of the challenges it faced on the continent:

By March 1961 the Congo was in turmoil; a number of the new states, especially Guinea, Mali, and Ghana, seemed well launched on the Marxist road; and most of the rest of Africa was consumed with bitterness toward the West. The Atlantic countries had never stood lower nor the Soviet Union higher in the minds of politically conscious Africans.[7]

Administration officials believed a new approach to Africa was needed. During the 1960 campaign, Kennedy had argued that "we have lost ground in Africa because we have neglected and ignored the needs and aspirations of the African people."[8] After his election, Kennedy's aides launched an energetic diplomatic effort to woo African leaders. Young, enthusiastic ambassadors were dispatched to the continent. A steady stream of African heads of state were welcomed in Washington: eleven in 1961, ten in 1962, and seven in 1963. Increased interest translated into increased aid. Between 1958 and 1962, Washington increased the flow of assistance to Africa from $110 million to $519 million (see figure 2.1). Over this brief span, aid to Africa increased from roughly 2 percent of total U.S. overseas aid to 8 percent.

Official interest in Africa waned as quickly as it had risen. "Africa," one scholar wrote in 1965, "has come to be an area of residual interest for the United States."[9] Washington's concern about the continent ebbed when U.S. officials realized that they had exaggerated the Communist threat there. African leaders' flirtations with the Soviet Union proved to be little more than a minor irritant. The economic and cultural ties binding the continent's fledgling states to Europe proved far more powerful than anything Moscow or Beijing (which had also displayed an interest in Africa in the early 1960s) could offer. The views of individuals such as Lyndon Johnson's under secretary of state for political affairs, George Ball, who had never taken the Communist threat in Africa very seriously, became predominant. ("We could," Ball wrote in his memoirs, "simplify our problems with Africa as well as with certain other areas of the less-developed world if we did not take such a proprietary interest in their development.")[10] By 1964, according to Anthony Lake, a former State Department official, it was "conventional bureaucratic wisdom that the Chinese and Russians would be unsuccessful in

FIGURE 2.1. U.S. AID TO AFRICA
1958 TO 1988

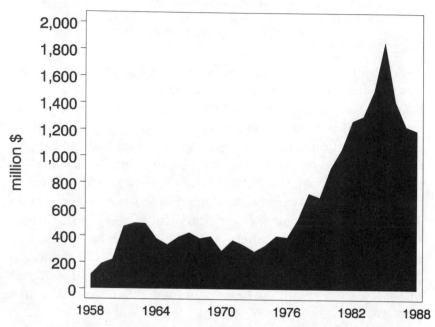

Source: Agency for International Development, *U.S. Overseas Loans and Grants and Assistance from International Organizations* (Washington, D.C.: Agency for International Development, miscellaneous years).

efforts to dominate the new nations of Africa; [and] the official perception of American interests in Africa dwindled accordingly."[11] During the final years of the Johnson presidency, Africa was, in the words of an unnamed official, "the last issue considered, the first aid budget cut."[12]

By the time Richard Nixon became president in 1969, he had forgotten his earlier exaggerated claim that Africa was a critical geopolitical testing ground. Instead, his administration's first annual report on foreign policy pointed to the continent as "one of the world's striking examples . . . of the failure of the appeal of communism in new nations."[13] Given this assessment, Nixon and his advisers saw no reason for the United States to undertake any significant initiatives on the continent. The phrase "Africa for the Africans," which some officials in the

Kennedy administration had used as a battle cry against the old Eurocentric orientation of U.S. policy, took on new meaning. It became a convenient rationale for benign, some would say malign, neglect. "If Africa is to move ahead in the 1970s," the president's foreign policy report of 1972 declared, "it must be largely on the basis of its own efforts and its own prescriptions."[14]

As interest in the continent declined, American financial assistance also dropped. Over the decade from 1963 to 1973, U.S. aid to Africa declined substantially in both absolute and relative terms. Total U.S. aid to Africa in 1973 ($286 million) equaled less than 60 percent of the total for 1963 ($519 million) (see figure 2.1).

In the mid-1970s, events in southern Africa caused U.S. officials to begin to pay attention to the continent again. As with its interest in Africa generally, Washington's interest in the countries of the racially divided southern tier has been under the strong influence of geopolitics. After a brief flurry of activity in the early 1960s, southern Africa—like the rest of the continent—had been largely forgotten. When Nixon and his national security adviser, Kissinger, took over the reins of power they formulated a policy of neglect based on two assumptions: that, as National Security Memorandum 39 of 1970 suggested, the whites were there to stay;[15] and that the Soviet Union would not intervene in the region. These assumptions were shattered in April 1974 when a group of young radical Portuguese colonels fed up with dictators and colonial wars staged a coup and precipitated the collapse of Portuguese colonial rule. A civil war broke out in Angola, one of Portugal's soon-to-be-independent colonies. Both superpowers were quickly drawn into the conflict, with the Soviet Union and Cuba backing one party—the Movimento Popular de Libertacao de Angola (MPLA)—and the United States backing two others—the Frente Nacional de Libertacao de Angola (FNLA) and the Uniao Nacional para a Independencia Total de Angola (UNITA).[16]

In explaining the Ford administration's decision to intervene in Angola, Secretary of State Kissinger left little doubt about his priorities: "America's modest direct strategic and economic interests in Angola are not the central issue. The question is whether America still maintains the resolve to act responsibly as a great power."[17] A failure to counter Moscow's moves in southern Africa could, Kissinger argued, encourage expansion elsewhere and cause our allies to question our will to defend them. Should foreign countries begin to doubt American resolve, he predicted, "we are likely to find a massive shift in the foreign policies of many countries and a fundamental threat over a period of time to the security of the United States."[18] If the Soviet factor had not been present, Kissinger and the rest of the foreign policy Establishment would not have cared which party came to power in Luanda.[19]

The MPLA's triumph in Angola placed Africa back on the geopolitical map. With startling rapidity, both superpowers intervened in conflicts across the continent. Soviet leaders sensed an opportunity to make good on their claims to strategic parity and shift the global "correlation of forces" in their favor.[20] U.S. policymakers, reeling from the American defeat in Vietnam, worried that Soviet successes might snowball.

In his final year as secretary of state, Kissinger became deeply involved in an effort to preempt further Soviet gains in southern Africa by negotiating the end of white rule in Rhodesia and Namibia and encouraging reform in South Africa. His efforts marked the beginning of a new phase in U.S. policy. Once again, aid levels shifted with the geopolitical tide. As figure 2.1 shows, U.S. aid to Africa increased dramatically from 1974 to 1984.

The United States was more active in Africa from the mid-1970s through the mid-1980s than at any time in its history. That this period of activity came after the Soviet Union had gained a foothold on the continent was not a coincidence. Despite widely varying ideological predispositions, all three administrations that governed during this period—Ford, Carter, and Reagan—determined their African priorities largely by geopolitical considerations. Throughout this period, U.S. officials were preoccupied with the fear that trends in southern Africa and the Horn of Africa, if ignored or mishandled, would benefit the Soviet Union. Even those officials who favored policies that were responsive to regional realities defended them in geopolitical terms. Former Secretary of State Cyrus Vance, for example, wrote in his memoirs, "The critical question was what politically and militarily feasible strategies would most effectively counter Soviet actions while advancing our overall interests."[21] This reality was never lost on the Africans themselves.

Following the Iranian revolution of 1979, President Jimmy Carter enunciated the so-called Carter doctrine, which committed the United States to use military means to defend American interests in the oil-rich Persian Gulf. This greatly increased the strategic importance of Kenya, Somalia, and Sudan, each of which could serve as a way station for troops and supplies headed for the Gulf. Figure 2.2, which shows the dramatic increase in U.S. aid to these countries, thus provides a good indicator of the extent to which geopolitics influenced the flow of resources into Africa.

FIGURE 2.2.   U.S. AID TO KENYA, SOMALIA, AND SUDAN
1974 TO 1988

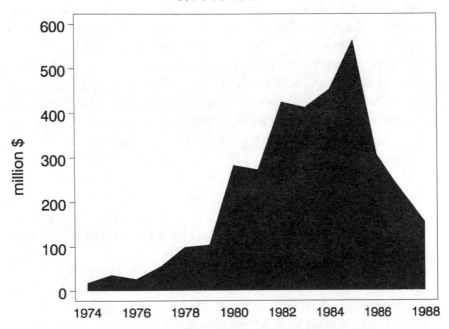

Source: Agency for International Development, *U.S. Overseas Loans and Grants and Assistance from International Organizations* (Washington, D.C.: Agency for International Development, miscellaneous years).

The Cold War ended in Africa on December 22, 1988, with the signing of a tripartite agreement clearing the way for the independence of Namibia, Africa's last colony, and the withdrawal of Cuban troops from Angola.[22] A mutual recognition on the part of Moscow and Washington that neither would gain from further competition in Africa facilitated this agreement. But signs that the competition between the superpowers was becoming less intense in Africa were evident considerably before the Namibia accord.

For the Soviet Union, a key turning point came in the early 1980s, when Moscow informed Mozambique, which had signed a treaty of friendship and cooperation with the Soviet Union in 1977, that it would not be invited to join the Council for Mutual Economic Assistance (COMECON) and suggested it seek economic assistance from the West.[23] By the mid-1980s, a consensus had formed among most students of Soviet policy toward Africa that Moscow was pulling back.[24] Only in Angola and Ethiopia, where the political costs of a precipitous withdrawal were likely to be high, did Soviet officials seem inclined to stand their ground; and in both of those places, the Soviet Union was on the defensive.

As the Soviet threat in Africa receded, some officials within the Reagan administration sensed an opportunity to reverse the gains that Moscow had made in the 1970s. They joined forces with some prominent conservative opinion leaders to champion the so-called Reagan doctrine, calling for aid to guerrillas fighting against Soviet-backed governments.[25] This coalition succeeded in winning support for Jonas Savimbi and UNITA, who had continued to fight the MPLA government in Luanda after they lost round one of the Angolan civil war. For the rest of Africa, however, a waning Soviet threat meant declining U.S. security assistance. (See figure 2.3.) The turnabout in U.S. priorities was most marked in the Horn of Africa. U.S. aid to countries there declined rapidly in the late 1980s. (See figure 2.2.)

With the Cold War over, the United States also lost the urge to intervene in African conflicts. This has been most obvious in Chad, Liberia, and Somalia, all of which were major recipients of U.S. military aid in the early 1980s. In Liberia, the Bush administration refused to intervene in a horrific civil war that led to the ouster of President Samuel Doe in September 1990. In Chad, U.S. officials hardly blinked when, in November 1990, rebel forces defeated another erstwhile client—Hissene Habre. The civil war in Somalia, which resulted in the January 1991 overthrow of Siad Barre, caused even fewer ripples in Washington. If the Soviet Union had still loomed on the horizon, the United States would not have been so passive. Instead, we would have probably witnessed interventions similar to those that occurred when rebel forces threatened President Mobutu Sese Seko in Zaire in the late 1970s or when Libya became involved in the civil war in Chad in the 1980s. It is also doubtful that the president and his advisers would have acquiesced so readily when Congress imposed reductions in aid to Kenya, Somalia, and Sudan if Soviet influence had still been perceived as a threat to U.S. interests in the Horn of Africa.

FIGURE 2.3.   U.S. MILITARY AID TO AFRICA
1974 TO 1988

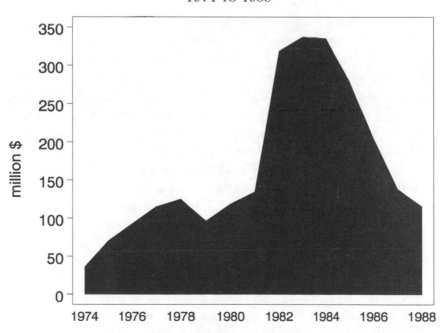

Source: Agency for International Development, *U.S. Overseas Loans and Grants and Assistance from International Organizations* (Washington, D.C.: Agency for International Development, miscellaneous years).

3

U.S. ECONOMIC INTERESTS IN AFRICA

One of the major reasons that shifting geopolitical currents so affect American policy toward Africa is the fact that the United States has few tangible interests there. The existence of significant, widely recognized economic and strategic interests—such as those the United States has in Western Europe, Japan, and the Persian Gulf states—directs and to a certain extent stabilizes policy. Clearly identifiable interests reduce the need for constant debate and reassessment and foster continuity from administration to administration. Where interests are limited or ambiguous, as in the case of Africa, policy is much more sensitive to the changing moods of U.S. domestic constituencies and the instinctive reactions of midlevel officials in Washington.

Since the mid 1950s, a number of commentators have argued that Africa is economically important to the United States. In 1956, Chester Bowles—a leading figure in the Democratic party who was the first prominent American politician to take an interest in Africa—wrote that the African "continent may turn out to be the richest in those natural resources that make our modern industrial age possible."[1] Two decades later, a manifesto on U.S. policy toward southern Africa issued by black American political leaders declared: "The African continent's vast mineral wealth includes all of the 53 critical minerals required for industrial expansion in the West. . . . U.S. trade with Africa is increasing faster than it is with other parts of the world. African nations are rapidly becoming important areas of American private investment."[2]

In 1988, another politician seeking to put the continent on the U.S. policy agenda (presidential candidate Jesse Jackson) emphasized that "Africa is a major source of strategic minerals, diamonds, gold, copper, and other resources important to the rest of the world."[3] American conservatives have been equally grandiloquent in discussing U.S. interests in Africa. For exam-

14

ple, former Central Intelligence Agency (CIA) official Ray Cline wrote in the late 1970s that "central and southern Africa is a geostrategic zone that is a rich treasure house of industrial raw materials—a prime target for the U.S.S.R. because of the area's political weakness and its crucial value as a trading partner for Western Europe, Japan, and the United States."[4]

Over the past three decades, official U.S. policy statements have routinely emphasized American economic interests in Africa. In August 1976, for example, Secretary of State Kissinger declared that Africa's "vast natural resources are essential elements of the global economy."[5] The following year, Anthony Lake, director of the State Department's policy planning staff, cited Africa's "growing importance to the United States and other industrial nations as a source of raw materials and oil."[6] Similar statements appear in almost every speech on Africa made by U.S. officials. It should not be surprising, therefore, that many Africans accept as orthodoxy the Leninist argument that economic interests drive U.S. policy toward their continent. By whatever measure one uses, however, American economic interests in Africa are marginal.

Exports to Africa have never accounted for a substantial proportion of total U.S. exports. U.S. imports from Africa did rise substantially in the 1970s, but this was almost entirely the result of a rise in oil prices and an increase in the volume of oil exported from Africa. By the late 1980s, U.S. imports from Africa had returned to their previously low levels. (See table 3.1.)

The impact of economic considerations on American policy

TABLE 3.1. U.S. TRADE WITH AFRICA
(Percent of U.S. total)

	1970	1975	1980	1985	1988
Imports	3	6	8	3	2
Exports	3	3	2	2	1

Source: International Monetary Fund, *Direction of Trade* (Washington, D.C.: International Monetary Fund, miscellaneous years).

toward the continent as a whole is further limited because U.S. economic interests there are concentrated in a very few countries. As figure 3.1 shows, two countries—Nigeria and South Africa—account for most of U.S. trade with Africa.

Another indicator of the relative insignificance of U.S. economic interest in Africa is the declining importance of U.S. trade there relative to U.S. trade with Asia and Latin America. (See figure 3.2.)

U.S. direct investment in Africa is also relatively unimportant. (See table 3.2.) No African nation ranks among the top twenty locations for U.S. investments. Total U.S. investment in sub-Saharan Africa currently equals less than one-third of U.S. investment in Brazil alone. Moreover, as with trade, U.S. investment in Africa is highly concentrated: mostly in South Africa and the oil-producing countries—especially Nigeria, Cameroon, Angola, and Gabon.

The need for access to strategic minerals has always been one of the major arguments used to prove Africa's economic importance to the United States and other industrial nations.[7] But this concern receded in the late 1980s for two reasons. First, dynamic models of mineral supply that take into account the role of market forces in encouraging exploration, conservation, and technological substitution have supplanted static analyses based on the distribution of already proven mineral reserves. The result has been a growing recognition that supplies of strategic minerals are not as limited as they once appeared.[8] Second, the argument that hostile states might deny mineral supplies to the United States and other Western powers has lost its credibility.[9] The experience of U.S. oil companies in Angola was particularly critical in discrediting this argument. Despite an ideologically hostile government with close ties to the Soviet Union, Angolan oil exports to the United States expanded significantly after independence in 1975. A good indication of the shift in thinking on strategic minerals came in June 1985, when Deputy Assistant Secretary of Defense Noel Koch, in one of the few speeches on Africa ever made by a senior Defense Department official, commented: "The value of [strategic] minerals is far more commer-

FIGURE 3.1. PRINCIPAL U.S. TRADING PARTNERS IN AFRICA, 1988

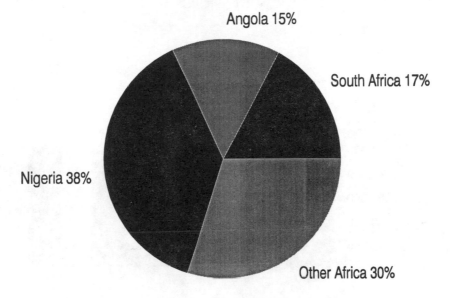

A. U.S. IMPORTS FROM AFRICA

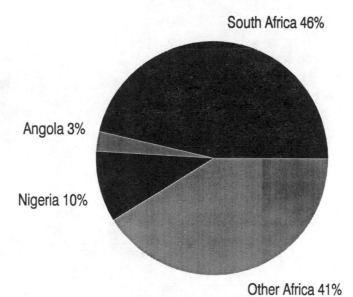

B. U.S. EXPORTS TO AFRICA

Source: International Monetary Fund, *Direction of Trade* (Washington, D.C.: International Monetary Fund, 1989).

FIGURE 3.2. U.S. TRADE WITH AFRICA, ASIA, AND LATIN AMERICA
1970 TO 1988

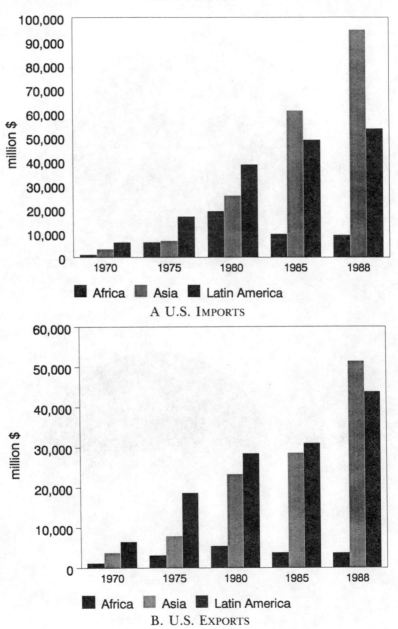

A U.S. IMPORTS

B. U.S. EXPORTS

Source: International Monetary Fund, *Direction of Trade* (Washington, D.C.: International Monetary Fund, miscellaneous years).

TABLE 3.2.   U.S. INVESTMENT IN LESS-DEVELOPED COUNTRIES
(LDCs), 1988

	Investment (billion $)	% of total
World	421	100
Sub-Saharan Africa	2	1
North Africa	4	1
Latin America	73	17
Asian LDCs	25	6

Source: "U.S. Direct Investment Abroad," *Survey of Current Business,* vol. 71, no. 6, June 1991.

cial than military, and far more prospective than real in the presently depressed mineral market. We should not wish to have our access to them denied. But there is not presently, nor foreseeably, a serious prospect of denial."[10]

In 1958, economist Andrew Kamarck predicted that "Africa as a source of raw materials and as a market for United States goods is destined to play a more important part in the American economy of the future."[11] In 1991, that economic promise remains unfulfilled; and U.S. economic interests in Africa remain marginal.

4

AMERICAN IMAGES AND AFRICAN REALITIES

In the absence of concrete interests, images become more important in the formulation of policy. Unfortunately, American perceptions of the African continent are shallow and highly skewed. A national survey taken in 1979 (one of the few ever to examine public attitudes toward Africa) asked "What comes to your mind when you think about Africa and the people who live there?" Some 25 percent of respondents mentioned animals and primitive natives, 37 percent mentioned racial issues, 16 percent mentioned poverty and hunger, and 14 percent failed to answer at all.[1] Many Africanists (individuals with a professional interest in African issues) blame the media for these negative, and largely uninformed, responses. There is considerable truth to this charge. As a number of studies have shown, the American media do not do a good job of covering Africa.[2] They regularly report bad news and seldom report good news. In South Africa, for example, American newspapers have focused on factional fighting among black groups, while largely ignoring the work of black community development groups, even though the groups engaged in community development are much more representative of black South Africa than the groups engaged in the fighting. Historically, Western authors have not done much better in presenting Americans with a balanced picture of African reality. As journalist Sanford Ungar pointed out, "From the earliest references in literature, both scholarly and popular, the continent suffered from the vision of 'darkest Africa'—a place of savages, jungles, and chaos."[3] Nevertheless, Africa's image cannot be ascribed solely to bad reporting. Three realities have made it difficult for many Americans to understand and relate to Africa.

REALITY 1: THERE IS NO "AFRICA"

Israel exists. Poland exists. Japan exists. Nicaragua exists. South Africa exists. They are places not abstractions. Americans can and do relate to them in concrete ways. "Africa" does not exist in a similar sense. People visit, work, and live in one of some fifty African countries, not in "Africa." American officials interact with officials from African countries, not the continent. This reality influences the way Americans relate generally to Africa.

Attitudes toward "Africa" are more ephemeral than attitudes toward specific countries; they fluctuate with changing intellectual and popular fashions. And they seldom reflect the tremendous diversity of the African continent. The continent's problems do have important common roots, but those roots are not what most Americans see when they are exposed to Africa.

Parts of Africa are potentially rich and prosperous; others are poor and likely to remain so for many years. Some areas are inviting and accessible; others are forbidding and inaccessible. How individual Americans perceive "Africa" will depend on which, if any, parts of the continent they have come into contact with. Each of the continent's seven identifiable regions has its own unique dynamic.

Southern Africa—Angola, Botswana, Lesotho, Malawi, Mozambique, Namibia, South Africa, Swaziland, Zambia, and Zimbabwe—has been a battleground for much of the post-independence period. While colonialism crumbled elsewhere in the 1960s and 1970s, in Angola, Mozambique, Namibia, Rhodesia (Zimbabwe), and South Africa, white rulers clung tenaciously to power. The result was long and bitter wars that engulfed the entire region and drew in the superpowers. Racial conflict became interwoven with ideological and geopolitical struggles. Economically, southern Africa, with rich mineral resources, fertile land, and the continent's only industrial economy, has tremendous potential.

Geographically, *the Horn of Africa* encompasses Djibouti, Ethiopia, and Somalia. In political terms, however, the Horn has expanded to include parts of Egypt, Kenya, Sudan, and Uganda. Like southern Africa, this region has been ravaged by war. Here, however, the causes have been religious and regional animosities; ideology has never been more than a tool to attract foreign support.

The countries of *East Africa*—Kenya, Tanzania, and Uganda—have little in common except former British colonial rule and coffee production. Despite very different economic and political systems, Kenya and Tanzania have been among the continent's most stable countries. Uganda has been one of the most conflict-ridden. The region has been much less affected by geopolitics than other parts of Africa.

At one time or another, most of the countries in *West Africa* and *Central Africa* have been ruled by military regimes. Since their independence, a majority of them have been locked in a tight economic relationship with their former colonial patron, France. Some of the coastal states have oil; others—especially the Sahelian states—have sand and not much else. Nigeria, in West Africa, is the continent's richest and most populous state.

North Africa—Algeria, Egypt, Libya, Morocco, and Tunisia—with its predominantly Muslim population, is more a part of the Middle East than of Africa. Its access to the Mediterranean Sea links it much more directly than the other regions to the European Community.

The *Indian Ocean Islands*—the Comoros Islands, Madagascar, Mauritius, and the Seychelles—are part of Africa by dint of their membership in the Organization of African Unity (OAU).

Differences among regions are thus considerable. There is no common language, religion, or culture. Because of the widely varying practices of imperial authorities in different colonies, even the legacy of colonialism divides existing African states and regions more than it links them. As a result, there is little continental interdependence. Trade among African nations is small. Events in Mozambique are largely irrelevant to Ghana; conflict in Liberia has no impact upon Malawi; Namibia's independence means little to the average Sudanese or Somali; and so on. These realities make it difficult to form the kind of stable and coherent image of "Africa" that would generate sustained interest by the American public.

REALITY 2: IT IS NOT CLEAR WHO
THE "AFRICANS" ARE

Among those Americans most sympathetic to Africans, there is considerable support for the idea that U.S. policy should be more sensitive to the diverse concerns and desires of Africans. The problem with this prescription is that just as there is no "Africa," there is also no monolithic group of "Africans" to whom Americans can refer.

In the early postindependence period, African governments were presumed to speak for their people. Ghana was Kwame Nkrumah. Tanzania was Julius Nyerere. Where "illegitimate" white-dominated governments existed, it was the leaders of the liberation movements who were treated as the spokesmen for the people. Today Africa speaks with many voices, and much of what is said is at odds with the words of official Africa. In wartorn countries—Angola, Ethiopia, Sudan, and others—opposition leaders can reasonably claim to represent more people than the governments. In relatively stable countries—Ivory Coast and Kenya are examples—the governments seem increasingly isolated from their constituents. Many young Africans dismiss Africa's elder statesmen—Kenneth Kaunda of Zambia and Nyerere of Tanzania, for instance—as tired and irrelevant.

Even in South Africa, where the issues seem clear and the heroes and villains obvious, it is not easy to decide who speaks for the Africans. During the U.S. debate over sanctions, for example, both advocates and critics of disinvestment argued that black South Africans supported their stance. Each side could quote prominent black leaders; and each side could cite numerous opinion polls. As a result, arguments over sanctions often degenerated into attacks and counterattacks on the credibility of different black leaders and groups within South Africa. Since Nelson Mandela's release from prison these arguments have intensified, with Jeane Kirkpatrick and other American conservatives championing the cause of Zulu leader Mangosuthu (Gatsha) Buthelezi, while antiapartheid activists and civil rights leaders embrace Mandela more fervently than ever.

The search for a single African voice that can guide Americans seeking to help the continent is both futile and dangerous—futile because, in Africa as elsewhere, sages and saviors too often prove incompetent, unpopular, or undemocratic; dangerous because attempts to anoint a leader (or group) usually spark bitter responses by the followers of other leaders (or groups). Witness the debate over the comparative merits and demerits of Jonas Savimbi, the Angolan guerrilla leader, whom many conservative spokesmen revere and most liberal commentators detest.

Africa, like the United States, has a diverse population with a wide variety of interests, opinions, and prejudices. Encouraging Americans to pay attention to what Africans think and want is a good idea. But it will not provide clear guidance for U.S. policymakers, since different Africans are likely to give widely disparate advice.

REALITY 3: THE NEWS FROM AFRICA HAS BEEN MOSTLY BAD

In the early 1960s, great hopes for rapid economic and political development throughout Africa sparked American interest in the continent. "Africa has greatness in her past as well as her present," declared the opening line of a book on the dawn of the independence era.[4] A desire to witness and participate in the heady business of building new nations drew academics, development experts, journalists, and political activists to the continent. Attractive, articulate, charismatic, and (mostly) young African leaders—Kaunda of Zambia, Jomo Kenyatta of Kenya, Nkrumah of Ghana, and Nyerere of Tanzania—reinforced the continent's appeal to the New Frontiersmen of the Kennedy era.

By the end of the decade, military coups and civil conflict had dampened the enthusiasm. Developments across the continent made Africa's booster club seem hopelessly naive. They also made it much easier for Presidents Johnson and Nixon to discount both Africa and Africanists. Calling the 1960s the "decade of disillusion," one analyst wrote:

> Events during the 1960s largely destroyed the euphoria aroused by independence, replacing expectancy with cynicism or resignation.

A score of regimes, created in the fine flush of anti-colonial nationalism, were unconstitutionally overthrown. . . . Instead of national prosperity . . . stagnation in the countryside, massive unemployment in the towns and ostentatious luxury for a tiny minority became the general experience. Detention without trial, public executions, inter-communal massacres commonly succeeded the colonial authoritarianism against which the nationalists had inveighed. . . . Corruption became rampant, graft commonplace.[5]

In the 1970s and 1980s, developments in Africa did little to dispel the pessimism that pervaded impressions of the continent in non-Africanist circles.[6] Among the most important and widely perceived negative trends were the demise of representative government; the proliferation of civil wars; the collapse of most African economies; a burgeoning refugee population; and, most recently, the horrifying AIDS crisis.

The dismal experiences of so many countries that Africanists had identified as examples of great promise has heightened negative perceptions of Africa. Ghana, the first black African nation to gain independence after World War II, became a textbook example of a failed democracy; and Nigeria, an emerging economic power of the 1970s, became an example of how easily and quickly oil wealth could be squandered. Mozambique, which many hailed as the most promising of the Afro-Marxist regimes that seized power in the 1970s, became the first to acknowledge the inability of strategies based on scientific socialism to transform African society.

The proliferation of bad news has had several results. It has discouraged U.S. businesses from investing in the continent; it has hampered American efforts to build public support for development assistance (as opposed to humanitarian relief); it has discouraged black Americans from identifying closely with the continent; it has discouraged academics and other professionals from embarking on careers focused on Africa; and it has discouraged ambitious mainstream U.S. politicians from making the continent their issue. In short, it has marginalized Africa.

5

U.S. DOMESTIC CONSTITUENCIES

The absence of a strong U.S. domestic constituency concerned with the continent has hampered efforts to strengthen American policy toward Africa. Writing in 1967, Professor Rupert Emerson cited "the lack of any widespread, coherent, and broadly based body of opinion which is seriously concerned with Africa" as one of the major difficulties confronting those who shape American policy toward Africa.[1] In 1973, Assistant Secretary of State David Newsom stated the problem rather bluntly in a speech to the African Studies Association: "One talks of a priority for Africa, but no administration can create a priority in foreign affairs that is not supported by a substantial segment of the American people."[2] Nearly three decades later, it is still not clear that powerful, enduring U.S. constituencies interested in Africa exist.

Africanists have become a small, politically isolated group with limited influence. Black Americans have long seemed a natural constituency for Africa; until 1990, however, their only decisive influence was on policy toward South Africa. Newer constituencies focused on issues such as famine relief, human rights, and the environment in Africa are just beginning to mature. To understand the potential strengths and weaknesses of these groups, we must examine each separately.

AFRICANISTS

In 1957, a group of thirty-five people, mostly scholars, gathered together in New York City to create the first professional association of Africanists: the African Studies Association (ASA). The ASA's founding members played a prominent role in the early debate over U.S. policy. Among the most prominent members to become involved in policymaking were L. Gray Cowan, the ASA's first executive secretary who later served as national intelligence officer for Africa in the Carter administration; Wayne Fredericks, a businessman who served as deputy assistant secretary of state under G. Mennen "Soapy" Williams; and Helen Kitchen, a journalist by training who has played a major informal advisory role in several administrations. President-elect Kennedy tapped several of those people, including Fredericks and Kitchen, to serve on a task force to make recommendations on new directions for U.S. foreign policy. A number were also appointed to a State Department advisory council on Africa established by Assistant Secretary of State Williams in 1961.

No other cohort of Africanists has been as involved in the policymaking process as was the first wave. This was no accident. The early Africanists were largely mainstream liberals, with a sprinkling of conservatives, such as Peter Duignan of the Hoover Institution. They were comfortable with the foreign policy Establishment; and the foreign policy Establishment, especially during the Kennedy years, was comfortable with them.

In the late 1960s and early 1970s, the political center in the Africanist community moved sharply to the left. Several forces caused this shift. The Vietnam war fostered strong tensions between the foreign policy Establishment and most academics working on Third World issues. The civil rights movement prompted black academics to question the preeminent influence of white scholars within the ASA. The cynical and disinterested way in which the Johnson and Nixon administrations dealt with African issues further alienated Africanists from official policymakers. The chasm widened throughout the 1960s as a growing number of academics embraced dependency theory—a theory of underdevelopment that blamed Western "neocolonialism" for the disappointing performance of independent Africa.

A turning point occurred at the 1969 ASA meeting in Montreal. During the meeting, a group of black scholars challenged the ASA's rules regarding membership and governance and demanded a greater role in running the organization. After their demands were rejected, the group walked out and formed a new group, the African Heritage Studies Association, which defined itself as part of a "worldwide decolonization movement."

The membership rules that prompted this split were soon amended, but the larger issues raised at Montreal lingered on.

Charges that "the ASA perpetuates colonialism and neo-colonialism"[3] put mainstream liberal scholars on the defensive. Complicating matters further was the fact that the CIA had played a major role in funding many African programs in the late 1950s and early 1960s. This funding created an atmosphere of suspicion. Any Africanist who had had dealings with the U.S. government risked coming under attack as a CIA agent. An article by an Africanist Idrian Resnick, written after Montreal, reflected the general mood of the times. In it Resnick argued that "Institutional ties with the U.S. government should be severed, for the Government's imperialist foreign policy in southern Africa and elsewhere should not be legitimized by Africanists."[4] Many scholars responded to these pressures by avoiding or reducing ties with official U.S. agencies; and many moderate and conservative students who were uncomfortable with the new orthodoxy simply avoided African studies.

By the end of the 1970s, the Africanist political spectrum was highly skewed to the political left. Until the Washington-based Heritage Foundation (not to be confused with the African Heritage Studies Association) and other right-wing think tanks made deliberate efforts to create their own cadres of African policy analysts, it was almost impossible to find conservatives who were knowledgeable about Africa. Those who could be found—Ned Munger of Cal Tech and Peter Duignan, for example—were treated as relics of the past and had no influence or protégés in the field.

A 1990 survey of ASA members confirmed the striking uniformity of Africanist opinion on U.S. policy.[5] Only 8 percent of those surveyed believed that long-term U.S. interests "are well served by current U.S. Africa policies." Fewer than 6 percent supported continued military aid to Kenya, Liberia, and Zaire. Fewer than 5 percent favored continued aid to Jonas Savimbi and UNITA. Moreover, 68 percent of respondents agreed that "access of Africanists to the U.S. policymaking process is limited to a small group of insiders," 28 percent were not sure, and only 4 percent disagreed. Most significantly, only 9 percent thought that "the Africanist community has been too confrontational in its approach to U.S. policy toward Africa."

The near-monolithic hostility of the Africanist community to official U.S. policy isolated it from the people who shape that agenda and influence Africa's place in it. This isolation became self-perpetuating in several ways. First, as the Africanist community tilted leftward, those who did not shift with it found themselves increasingly out of place at Africanist gatherings. Second, as so many Africanists chose to position themselves outside of the mainstream, the Establishment's gatekeepers—for example, those who solicit policy advice and recruit talent for television news shows—grew wary of interacting with them. As a result, university-based African experts have been much less visible—and hence much less influential—than their colleagues who work on other regions of the globe; and activist organizations such as the American Committee on Africa, which once attracted the support of prominent political figures, have ended up on the fringes of American politics.

The end of the Cold War has lessened the tension between government officials and Africanists. A new wave of younger, less ideological scholars (with no memories of Montreal and the Vietnam-era debates) is emerging. This group is more similar to the Africanist generation of the early 1960s than to the generation of the 1970s. But there is little prospect of a return to the "golden era" of the early 1960s when Africanists played a significant (albeit far from central) role in promoting interest in Africa within official circles. Africanists as a group are too small in number and too politically inconsequential to compete in the foreign policy arena of the 1990s.

AFRICAN-AMERICANS

Since the United States began to show interest in Africa, many analysts have predicted that American blacks would become the principal constituency for better U.S. relations with Africa. In 1967, Professor Emerson wrote that "The most vital and unique concern of the United States with Africa derives from the existence of that 10 percent of the American population which

. . . traces its ancestry to Africa."[6] In 1970 historian C. Erik Lincoln boldly prophesied that "As the American Negro grows more vocal, as it becomes more politically powerful, and as its identification with the struggles of emergent Africa and Asia is strengthened by the mutual recognition of one common problem—color—the Negro minority is destined to become an important counterweight to the traditional racial tone which has in the past characterized our foreign policy."[7] And in 1976 Anthony Lake observed that "in the absence of dramatic events in southern Africa which force a policy change, the direction U.S. policy takes [there] will depend heavily on the black community here. It is the only American group with both the inherent motive and the political means of forcing such a shift."[8] These predictions have been borne out, but only in part.

Since the early 1970s, African-Americans have become much more involved in influencing and formulating U.S. policy toward Africa. Politicians and policymakers now worry about the reactions of the black community to official U.S. statements and initiatives vis-à-vis Africa. But the depth and durability of black Americans' interest in U.S. policy toward the continent is still uncertain.

Given the realities outlined in Chapter 4, it should not be surprising that blacks have not universally embraced Africa. As Tilden LeMelle, a leading African-American Africanist, has pointed out, black Americans are not ethnic immigrants with relatively recent contacts to their lands of origin.[9] One indicator of changing black attitudes toward Africa over time is the use of self-designations that closely identify black Americans with the continent, such as African-American or Afro-American, as compared with race-based terms, such as "black," "Negro," or "colored." The fluctuating popularity of terms such as African-American has been directly related to developments on the continent. In the early 1960s, when Africa's image was improving, their popularity rose. In the late 1960s, as optimism about Africa faded, their popularity fell. In the late 1980s, a group of black leaders made a deliberate decision to identify themselves as African-Americans. This decision was prompted by the way in which South Africa captured the interest of black Americans when the struggle against apartheid dramatically intensified in 1984–85.[10] Whether or not most black Americans (a majority of whom still prefer to be called black)* go along with their leadership on this question will depend largely on what happens in Africa. If South Africa becomes a peaceful, nonracial democracy and the rest of the continent moves in a similar direction, more and more black Americans are likely to identify themselves as African-Americans. Regardless of how they identify themselves, however, Americans whose ancestors were born in Africa have consistently shown greater interest in that continent than Americans whose ancestors were born on other continents.

Polls taken as long ago as the late 1950s indicated that blacks were more inclined than whites to favor increased aid to Africa. In 1957, for example, one survey found that 56 percent of blacks favored U.S. efforts to help Africa as opposed to only 39 percent of whites.[11] Similarly, in a survey conducted in 1965, 33 percent of blacks agreed that the United States should spend most of its aid money on Africa, as opposed to only 10 percent of whites.[12] In a 1979 survey, when asked which of four areas—Europe, Asia, Africa, or Latin America—they were most interested in, 33 percent of blacks mentioned Africa, as opposed to only 4 percent of whites.[13] In contrast, 21 percent of blacks and 37 percent of whites chose Europe, while 14 percent of blacks and 33 percent of whites chose Asia. More recent surveys on general interest in Africa are not available, but substantial polling has taken place on South Africa, and it also evidences a greater interest in African issues among blacks than whites. For example, in February 1990, 60 percent of American blacks said they were closely following stories concerning Nelson Mandela's release from prison, as opposed to 30 percent of whites.[14]

A survey of eighty prominent U.S. black leaders conducted by the Joint Center for Political and Economic Studies in early 1990 provided a more detailed (and somewhat ambivalent) picture of black attitudes toward Africa.[15] In this survey, 90 percent

---

* A 1990 study by the Joint Center for Political and Economic Studies found that 72 percent of those surveyed preferred to be called black, 15 percent African-American, 3 percent Afro-American, 2 percent Negro, with the rest giving no opinion or other responses. See the *New York Times*, January 29, 1991, p. A19.

of the interviewees agreed that "black political leaders have a special obligation to influence U.S. foreign policy on behalf of Africa"; 59 percent said that their own interest focused on Africa. At the same time, however, only 24 percent mentioned "more focus on Africa" when asked to recommend one major change in U.S. foreign policy. A majority (56 percent) agreed that black Americans should be more concerned about Africa than about other world areas, but a substantial minority (41 percent) disagreed. Significantly, 47 percent of the respondents agreed that "very few black Americans feel any real close connection to Africa."

The strongest impulse for a concerted effort to mobilize black Americans to support Africa has come from intellectuals and political activists.[16] For example, W. E. B. Du Bois showed considerable interest in Africa long before it was fashionable to do so. In 1937, he helped to create the Council on African Affairs, which focused largely on South Africa. The first effort to organize a black lobby on Africa occurred in 1962 when Roy Wilkins, Martin Luther King, Jr., and other civil rights leaders formed the American Negro Leadership Conference on Africa (ANLCA). They were motivated by a belief that, in the words of Wilkins, "the not inconsiderable abilities we American Negro citizens possess should be harnessed in an effective fashion to . . . [persuade] our government to aid the emerging peoples of Africa toward their place in the world of nations."[17] Some officials in the Africa bureau of the State Department favored and even encouraged the emergence of a strong black lobby, hoping it would become a useful political ally, but senior officials did not share their views. In fact, the Johnson administration actively opposed the idea. "We're quite concerned," two NSC staff members wrote in March 1965, "over the prospect of an imminent Negro leadership conference to set up an organization to influence U.S. policy on Africa. As I recall the President's view, this is just what he *doesn't* want."[18]

The ANLCA failed to have much of an impact, but the idea of forming a black lobby on foreign policy continued to gain support. Representative Charles Diggs, a black congressman from Detroit, played a key role in keeping this idea alive. In 1976, he joined with Andrew Young to convene a black leadership conference on U.S. policy toward southern Africa. Out of this conference came a decision to form TransAfrica, a Washington-based organization set up to ensure that black Americans have a voice in foreign policy debates.

Under the leadership of Randall Robinson, TransAfrica quickly won the support of black political elites across the country. Robinson's links to Capitol Hill and the support of the Congressional Black Caucus helped TransAfrica to become an important force in Congress very quickly, but its public prominence and influence grew much more slowly. Most Americans had never heard of Robinson and TransAfrica until he organized a protest against apartheid outside the South African embassy in November 1984. That demonstration sparked a prairie fire of demonstrations across the country and led to the passage of the Comprehensive Anti-Apartheid Act of 1986. It also garnered Robinson recognition as an authoritative representative of African-American attitudes toward Africa.

TransAfrica's role in the antiapartheid movement aside, the dramatic shift that occurred in U.S. policy toward South Africa between 1984 and 1986 was due largely to the growing political influence of African-Americans. By 1984, the importance, both actual and perceived, of the black electorate had increased tremendously. Between 1972 and 1984, the proportion of black members of standing committees of the Democratic National Committee increased from 11 percent to 18 percent. More important, Jesse Jackson's surprisingly successful 1984 presidential campaign made politicians from both major parties keenly sensitive to black concerns. In a TransAfrica issue brief devoted to the 1984 presidential election, the editors observed: "Despite the black community's historical and growing interest in Africa and the Caribbean, issues relating to these regions have been among those least discussed—if they have not been ignored altogether—during a presidential campaign. . . . " Noting their success in soliciting responses to questions on policy toward Africa from Democratic candidates, the editors went on to say: "Perhaps the growing realization of the strength and centrality of the black electorate has been demonstrated by the willingness of the current presidential candidates to break with previous patterns of failing to address black world issues."[19]

Between 1984 and 1986, Republican leaders—including Jack Kemp and Newt Gingrich—who unexpectedly began to back sanctions legislation in the mid-1980s openly acknowledged the link between their posture on South Africa and their desire to end the Democratic near monopoly of support among blacks. Democrats were less open about the political-racial calculations behind their sudden enthusiasm for sanctions, but that did not change the reality.

The Reverend Leon Sullivan, a black minister and civil rights leader from Philadelphia who helped to put the apartheid issue on the U.S. corporate agenda in the 1970s, has recently launched a new initiative aimed at increasing African-American ties with the continent. In April 1991, a delegation of prominent African-American leaders headed by Sullivan attended the first "African–African American summit" in Abidjan. Its goal was "to propose a plan to assist with the development of Africa, and which will include strategies for creating closer cooperation between Africans and African Americans, and better American and African relations for support of Africa."[20] This initiative differs from previous ones—such as the ANLCA and Trans-Africa—in emphasizing economics instead of racial issues. Africare, a highly regarded black-led development organization, is working on similar initiatives.

Mobilizing black America to oppose white racism in southern Africa is much easier than creating an enduring American constituency for black Africa. Black America's large domestic agenda limits its ability to take on the additional burdens of Africa. Moreover, it is not clear that a consensus exists among black leaders on African issues. While there is significant black support for increased aid to Africa, there is no consensus on who should receive that aid and for what purposes.

It is also not clear that the growing tendency of U.S. politicians and many establishment institutions, especially some of the major foundations, to view African issues as exclusively "black" issues serves either African or African-American interests.[21] Defining African issues in these terms reinforces the view that the

United States has no national (as opposed to ethnic) interests in Africa. This creates a danger that U.S. policymaking will be reduced to an ad hoc and often merely symbolic effort to satisfy black constituencies. Other potentially significant constituencies could be discounted in the process, and nonblacks may be discouraged from becoming involved with Africa. A danger also exists that African-Americans will gain greater influence over policy toward Africa at the cost of broader inclusion in the overall foreign policy process. Implicitly, the argument that African-Americans have a greater claim on policy toward Africa than other people suggests that they have a lesser claim on policy toward other parts of the world.

What is required instead is a strategy that will enhance the concern of African-Americans with the continent without further marginalizing either Africa or African-Americans in the U.S. foreign policy process. Such a strategy would emphasize the importance of deepening ties between African-Americans and Africa as part of a broader strategy of creating society-to-society linkages between the United States and Africa.

ISSUE-ORIENTED CONSTITUENCIES

With the exception of the role African-Americans play in the debate over South Africa, the most important influence on U.S. policy toward Africa has come from groups that are not interested in the continent per se. These are constituencies concerned about particular issues or causes that happen to involve Africa, including human rights, development, women's rights, population, relief, and the environment. The strength of such constituencies is based on several common traits:

- A commitment to the promotion of a single, widely endorsed goal—for example, opposing political repression, feeding starving peoples, saving the planet—that can be expressed in powerful emotional terms;

- A mix of organizations with diverse political orientations and affiliations concerned about the same issue;

- A grass-roots base of supporters who regularly attend meetings, contribute funds, write letters, and so on;

- Well-organized national offices with effective public information, media, and lobbying operations and close working relationships with key members of Congress;

- A sophisticated network of global relationships linking them with other private groups and international organizations;

- The support of prominent entertainment personalities who are willing to serve as spokespersons and participate in high-profile fund-raising and consciousness-raising events.

Foreign policy constituencies organized around specific issues are a relatively new phenomenon. Prior to World War II, the groups that were most concerned with foreign policy were motivated principally by either economic or ethnic interests; the groups that formed in the first half of the twentieth century to campaign for world government were an exception. Of the constituencies that are now most interested in Africa, the first to emerge was the relief community.

Relief agencies, organized primarily by churches and immigrant associations, emerged in response to the ravages of the two world wars. Since the 1960s, this community has broadened considerably to include a kaleidoscopic assortment of local and national organizations. (See table 5.1.) Many of these belong to the American Council for Voluntary International Action, more commonly known as InterAction, a coalition formed in 1984 to serve as a vehicle for cooperation among private voluntary organizations and as liaison between these organizations and official agencies.[22] Although it is not a lobby per se, InterAction has become an important voice in debates concerning relief and development.

The human rights movement began to grow in the 1960s, but it did not become a strong domestic political force until the mid-1970s.[23] Four major national organizations concerned with human rights now have significant African programs: Africa Watch, Amnesty International, the Lawyers' Committee for Human Rights, and the Southern Africa Project of the Lawyers'

TABLE 5.1. MAJOR U.S. RELIEF ORGANIZATIONS

Organization	Date Created	Budget (million $)	Number of African Countries Served
Adventist Development and Relief International	1956	32	23
Africare	1971	13	21
American Friends Service Committee	1917	19	7
American Red Cross	1881	978	
AmeriCares	1979	59	10
CARE	1945	358	16
Catholic Relief Services	1943	220	29
Christian Children's Fund	1938	92	8
Church World Service	1946	39	29
Food for the Hungry	1970	27	5
Heifer Project	1944	10	8
Helen Keller International	1915	6	12
International Rescue Committee	1933	25	2
Lutheran World Relief	1945	26	13
Mennonite Central Committee	1920	26	17
National Council of Negro Women	1935	3	7
Oxfam	1970	11	15
Save the Children	1932	78	11
World Vision	1950	143	26
YMCA	1889	25	10

Source. InterAction, *Member Profiles* (New York: InterAction, May 1989).

Committee for Civil Rights under Law. They have played leading roles in congressional debates on Kenya, Liberia, Somalia, Sudan, and Zaire.

Despite its long historical roots, the American environmental movement became an important foreign policy constituency only in the 1980s, and Africa was not an important priority except in the area of wildlife preservation.[24] But it is becoming more important as Greenpeace, the Audubon Society, and the Natural Resources Defense Council, among others, successfully lobby Congress to make environmental protection a priority in aid programming. Given the broad membership bases and the extensive public education programs of these groups, as they pay more attention to Africa, they will have a major influence on American perceptions of the continent.

The end of the Cold War will increase the influence of issue-oriented constituencies. In the past, their ability to affect policy depended on the extent to which their efforts coincided with U.S. geopolitical interests. In cases where relief efforts and human rights projects were consistent with the policy of containment, the president and Congress supported them. In cases where they were not, Washington opposed them. With the apparent demise of the Soviet threat, this constraint has been removed and the ability of relief agencies, human rights organizations, and environmental groups to influence the U.S. foreign policy agenda has been enhanced.

In discussing potential constituencies for Africa, it is important not to ignore the role of conservative organizations. In the 1960s and early 1970s, the most prominent conservative voices on Africa were southerners, mostly Democrats, in Congress— for example, Senator Harry Byrd of Virginia, who identified strongly with whites in Rhodesia and South Africa.[25] They led the fight for passage of the "Byrd amendment" of 1971, which placed the United States in violation of United Nations sanctions against Ian Smith's rebellious white minority government in southern Rhodesia. Until the mid-1970s, however, most conservatives did not pay much attention to Africa.

Soviet interventions in Angola (1975) and Ethiopia (1977) greatly increased conservative interest in Africa. The principal concerns of Senator Byrd and his allies had been racial, not strategic or ideological. In the late 1970s, opposition to communism and Soviet adventurism supplanted racism as the chief motive behind conservative interest. This shift had a number of effects. It caused conservatives to pay attention to black Africa. It forced them to develop policy positions that could not be discredited as racist. It encouraged them to seek out black African allies such as Bishop Abel Muzorewa in Zimbabwe, Jonas Savimbi in Angola, and Chief Buthelezi in South Africa. The result was a conservative stance on Africa (emphasizing strategic and ideological issues) that had considerably more political appeal in the United States than the old-style racism of the Byrd coalition.

In short, while it is probably still correct that, as Sanford Ungar observed in 1978, "only a small minority of Americans . . . pay careful attention to Africa,"[26] the number of those who do pay attention is growing, and they are becoming more outspoken. Moreover, their ability to influence policy has been enhanced by the domestic political changes discussed in Chapter 6, and it could be enhanced further by the global trends discussed in Chapter 9.

6

CHANGING AMERICAN REALITIES

Most Africanists and African-Americans strongly believe that Africa receives far less attention and far fewer resources than it deserves because of the foreign policy Establishment's inherent bias against the continent, a bias that they allege is rooted in racism. These charges contain some truth. But the problem is far more complex than most Africanists have been willing to admit. The foreign policy Establishment's experiences with—and predispositions toward—Africa have changed markedly over the past three decades. Moreover, the influence of that Establishment over Africa policy is neither as great nor as invariably negative as Africanists assume. Congress now plays an important and often decisive role; as a result, policy toward the continent has become a struggle between members of Congress allied with leaders of the various constituencies concerned with Africa and officials in the executive branch directly responsible for African issues.

THE FOREIGN POLICY ESTABLISHMENT
AND AFRICA

The elite community that shaped foreign policy throughout most of the post–World War II period consisted almost entirely of white males with little experience or interest in Africa.[1] Most members of this community had a natural affinity—ethnic, cultural, economic—for Europe. Many had had some exposure to Asia, Latin America, or the Near East. This state of affairs was largely a consequence of geography and history. In contrast to Great Britain, France, and the other European powers, the United States never had any African colonies. It never established a substantial presence on the continent; and it never developed an Africanist cadre of foreign service officers and economic agents. Additionally, until the 1960s, Americans generally had few opportunities or reasons to study, much less travel to, Africa.[2] (In 1959, for example, only 4,809 Americans visited South Africa, and that was three times the number that visited any other country or territory south of the Sahara.)[3]

Had pre-1960 contacts between the United States and Africa been different, U.S. opinion leaders might have developed a more informed and sympathetic attitude toward the continent. Given the history of limited interaction, their indifference is not surprising. It is a mistake, however, to focus on old realities. A new foreign policy community is emerging that includes many individuals with significant knowledge of and experience in Africa. These individuals are the product of several developments that began in the late 1950s and 1960s:

- Attracted by the unique opportunity to witness the birth of nations, scholars flocked to independent Africa to teach and do research;

- Thousands of idealistic college graduates joined the newly created Peace Corps and were sent to Africa;

- Many young journalists got a taste of Africa for the first time covering the civil wars in the Belgian Congo and Nigeria;

- Foreign service officers, aid workers, cultural attachés, and intelligence operatives were dispatched to staff embassies in the newly independent countries;

- Black Americans began to seek ways to build cultural links between black America and Africa.

Many of the people who moved into important positions in the foreign policy Establishment over the past decade had thus been exposed to Africa. Former Secretary of Defense and National Security Adviser Frank Carlucci was posted to Africa during his early days in the foreign service; the current president of the Council on Foreign Relations, Peter Tarnoff, began his career as a political officer in the U.S. embassy in Lagos, Nigeria; the managing editor of the *New York Times*, Joseph Lelyveld, served two stints as a foreign correspondent in South Africa; Joseph Nye, a Harvard professor of international relations and former foreign policy adviser to presidential candidate Michael Dukakis, wrote a book on regional integration in East Africa; and Arnaud de Borchegrave, managing editor of the *Washington Times*, worked for many years as a correspondent for *Newsweek* in Africa.

The racial complexion of the foreign policy Establishment is also changing. African-Americans are, at long last, starting to assume prominent positions in and out of government. In addition to selecting Andrew Young to be the principal U.S. representative to the United Nations, President Jimmy Carter appointed several blacks to key foreign policy posts, including Donald McHenry, who succeeded Young at the UN, and Goler Butcher, who headed the Africa bureau of the Agency for International Development. More recently, General Colin Powell has served as national security adviser and chairman of the Joint Chiefs of Staff, and Ambassador Edward Perkins has occupied the top professional post (director-general) in the Foreign Service. One indicator of the growing role of African-Americans in the foreign policy Establishment is the increase in the number of black members of the Council on Foreign Relations. Throughout the 1960s, only 10 blacks were elected to Council membership; this number increased to 47 in the 1970s, and to 97 in the 1980s.[4] African-American employment in the Foreign Service has followed a similar pattern. In 1960, the State Department had roughly 30 black career officers; by 1990 it had 279.[5]

The foreign policy Establishment's understanding of and sympathy for Africa has increased as growing numbers of African-Americans and individuals with experience in Africa climb up the rungs of the Establishment ladder. But this does not mean it will give greater priority to African issues. A far more important factor in determining whether or not the Establishment takes an interest in the continent will be the debate over America's role in the post-Cold War world. (See Chapter 8.) If, as now seems possible, most American opinion leaders conclude that developments in Africa will not significantly affect our larger geopolitical interests, the Establishment's interest in assuming a leading role in shaping policy toward the continent will decline even further than it has already. Instead, policy debates will pit segments of the foreign policy bureaucracy against members of Congress and a host of domestic constituencies concerned with African issues.

THE FOREIGN POLICY BUREAUCRACY AND AFRICA

Recognizing the difference between the interests of senior administration officials* and those of the midlevel officials (careerists and noncareerists) who have responsibility for policy toward specific regions and issues is crucial to understanding the political processes that determine U.S. policy toward Africa. Senior officials can be divided into two groups. Most of those concerned with foreign policy are drawn from the Establishment described above. They are usually generalists who focus on the overall direction of foreign policy rather than on specific issues and regions. The other important group consists of individuals such as the White House Chief of Staff who are primarily concerned with domestic politics. They are more interested in the domestic implications of foreign policies than in their substantive merits or international consequences. Neither of these two groups has a necessary or inherent interest in seeing the United States play an active role in Africa. In past administrations, both groups have usually considered problems on the continent to be a distraction.†

The interests of administration Africanists (officials who have responsibility for African issues in the various executive branch departments) are quite different from those of senior administration officials. Their power and status depends on the level of U.S. involvement in the continent's affairs. When the

* Senior administration officials would include the president, his chief of staff, cabinet members (especially the secretary of state and the secretary of defense), the national security adviser, and, in some administrations, the principal U.S. representative to the United Nations. It also includes deputy secretaries and under secretaries. Lesser officials who work directly for these officials—for example, executive assistants, personal counsels, staff assistants, and so on—also usually share the perspective of the senior officials for whom they work.

†There have been a few notable exceptions to this generalization. They include Chester Bowles, a prominent Democratic party leader who served as undersecretary of state in the Kennedy administration; Adlai Stevenson, a two-time Democratic party presidential candidate who served as U.S. Ambassador to the United Nations from 1961 to 1964; Cyrus Vance, who served as secretary of state in the Carter administration; and, to a somewhat lesser extent, George Shultz, who served as secretary of state from 1983 to 1989.

United States is greatly involved in Africa, they are more powerful and important; when the United States is less involved, their status diminishes. These officials, especially the assistant secretary of state for African affairs, regularly advocate expanding the official presence of the United States on the continent; and they almost always argue that linkages exist between developments in Africa and the administration's ability to realize larger foreign policy objectives. Conversely, they seldom argue that American interests would be served by limiting or reducing official U.S. involvement, or admit that what happens in Africa may be geopolitically inconsequential. The predictability of their views on such issues is one of the reasons that senior officials—and the foreign policy Establishment more generally—are often skeptical of arguments made by government specialists on Africa.

Officials with regional responsibilities must work within limits set by senior officials. Arguments that African issues are intrinsically important to the United States seldom carry the day on the seventh floor of the State Department or at the White House. The most successful Africanists are those who are able to persuade their superiors that African issues are important in global terms. For example, Assistant Secretary of State for African Affairs Richard Moose and other officials concerned with Africa in the Carter administration maintained high-level support for their southern African initiatives by arguing that those efforts would limit opportunities for Soviet expansion in the Third World and enhance the credibility of the U.S. commitment to global human rights, both of which were high administration priorities. Similarly, Assistant Secretary Chester Crocker won approval of his effort to broker a settlement in Namibia from Secretary of State Alexander Haig and President Reagan by arguing that it offered a way to reverse Soviet and Cuban gains in the Third World.[6]

In theory, strong domestic constituencies interested in Africa should provide administration Africanists with political allies and hence strengthen their bargaining power vis-à-vis senior administration officials. In practice, however, the relationship between those in government who deal with African issues and groups outside of government interested in policy toward the continent is usually strained.

Close ties with academics, African-Americans, and other constituencies outside of government can be a liability for mid-level officials. Such ties can be construed (or misconstrued) within an administration as evidence that an official has been "captured" by groups that do not share the administration's "broader" perspective on international issues. For example, the fact that Donald Easum, who served as assistant secretary of state for African affairs in 1973–74, was known to listen to and sympathize with Africanists outside of government hurt his standing with Secretary of State Kissinger. This dilemma exists for all midlevel officials concerned with foreign policy issues, but it is most severe for those concerned with Africa because, as Chapter 5 documented, the constituencies concerned with Africa tend to be uniformly critical of administration policies even when the administration is favorably inclined toward the continent.

But the fundamental source of tension between administration Africanists and U.S. constituencies concerned with Africa derives from the mutual and irreconcilable desire of both groups to control policy. The first priority of all officials is to protect and enhance their influence; strengthening constituency groups serves that interest only so long as the constituencies support the policies the officials favor. Similarly, cooperating with officials is useful for constitutent groups only so long as the officials adopt policies the constituencies prefer. When constituencies are weak, they are often eager for access and thus willing to follow the bureaucrats' lead. As they grow stronger, they become more independent and demanding, thus increasing the chances of clashes. The strongest constituencies often choose to circumvent the midlevel bureaucracy and deal directly with senior administration officials.

The evolution of relations between black Americans and administration Africanists has followed this pattern. In the early 1960s, Assistant Secretary of State Soapy Williams and his deputy, Wayne Fredericks, actively sought to get black leaders in the United States to speak out on African issues. Given the weakness of that constituency, Williams had no reason to fear that it would turn against him. But its weakness also meant it was not a very useful ally. As the black constituency interested in Africa has become more powerful and active, relations between the State Department's Africanists and black leaders have become more strained. In the Carter era, black leaders were often critical of administration policy toward southern Africa, even though the administration's position on such issues differed only marginally from the views of most black leaders. During the Reagan era, Assistant Secretary Crocker frequently clashed with members of the Congressional Black Caucus and other black organizations, especially over policy toward southern Africa. His successor— Herman Cohen—has reduced tensions, largely because he seems to have recognized political reality and deliberately avoided taking public positions that would antagonize important black congressional leaders.

Similar tensions exist between administration Africanists and the academic community. The Department of State's Bureau of African Affairs and the various branches of the intelligence community frequently hold conferences and hire academic consultants with the ostensible objective of soliciting expert advice. These exercises seldom, if ever, have an impact on official thinking. Except for occasional and brief ceremonial appearances, senior officials almost never participate. In fact, the agenda and speakers are almost always organized in a way that ensures that administration assumptions and policies are not subjected to effective challenges. Often the main purpose of these meetings is to defuse potential critics or enhance the prestige of those responsible for arranging the exchanges.* While the contacts that grow out of these exercises may benefit individual analysts and academics, they rarely affect policy.

Administration Africanists almost always resist attempts by

* A clear example of the way this process works is the Defense Intelligence Agency's ongoing effort to court the Africanist academic community. When this effort was conceived in the early 1980s, the DIA's African analysts were generally perceived within the foreign policy community as more conservative and less expert than their counterparts in the Central Intelligence Agency and the Department of State's Bureau of Intelligence and Research. Although the stated objective of the DIA outreach effort was to improve the agency's African analytical capabilities, an equally (if not more) important unstated objective was to boost DIA's reputation vis-à-vis other parts of the official Africanist community.

other groups outside of the executive branch to play a greater role in the policymaking process; senior officials, however, often accommodate such groups, provided they can do so in a way that does not limit their freedom to deal with issues they regard as more important. For senior officials who have no personal interest in maintaining control over policy toward Africa, the stakes are seldom worth the risk of domestic battles. In fact, they often undercut their own Africanists at the first sign of political trouble. This process was at work in 1985–86 when the Reagan administration largely abandoned Assistant Secretary of State Crocker and his strategy of constructive engagement when he came under attack from both conservatives and liberals.

Recognizing the difference between the interests of senior officials and official Africanists helps to explain a seeming contradiction in the Bush administration's policies toward southern Africa. On the issue of sanctions against South Africa, the Bush administration resisted calls to lift sanctions (as a reward to President F. W. de Klerk for the steps he has taken to end apartheid) for much longer than most analysts expected. The administration also continued to provide covert arms and assistance to Jonas Savimbi and UNITA far longer than most analysts expected. In both cases, the administration adopted the course of action that would least antagonize powerful domestic constituencies. On the apartheid issue, the pro-sanctions constituency was far more potent than the anti-sanctions constituency. On the Angolan issue, the pro-Savimbi constituency was far more potent than the anti-Savimbi constituency. On both issues, the Africa bureau of the State Department preferred a different tilt.

During the administration's internal debates, Assistant Secretary of State Cohen argued that the United States should offer President de Klerk some tangible rewards for his efforts. At the same time, Cohen (like his predecessor) is believed to be more willing than his superiors to twist Savimbi's arm to achieve a settlement in Angola. In both cases, the assistant secretaries' personal interests differ from the political interests of senior administration officials. President Bush will not receive any significant domestic political dividends from lifting sanctions. Nor has his administration suffered because it lagged behind other industrial powers in doing so. In contrast, lifting sanctions may boost Assistant Secretary Cohen's standing with Pretoria and allow him to get more closely involved in the transformation that is underway in South Africa. Similarly, with Cuba and the Soviet Union already on their way out of southern Africa, President Bush will derive few benefits from the negotiated settlement in Angola, especially if it does not put Savimbi into power. But his assistant secretary's personal reputation and influence in Africa has been somewhat enhanced by the agreement that was signed in Lisbon in June 1991.

Over the past decade, the growing assertiveness of the U.S. Congress has increased the potential importance of bureaucratic tension between senior officials and official Africanists. When Congress and important domestic constituencies ignore Africa, senior officials have little reason to question or limit the prerogatives of their Africanist deputies. As Congress and others begin to pay greater attention to Africa, those officials have to worry more about their deputies' actions becoming a political liability.

THE INCREASING IMPORTANCE OF CONGRESS

The growing role of Congress in foreign policymaking has had a tremendous impact on U.S. policy toward Africa. Throughout the 1960s, Congress showed little interest in Africa. Writing in 1976, Anthony Lake observed that "American policy toward southern Africa consists, and will continue to consist, far more of actions and statements decided by the executive branch without formal reference to the legislature."[7] Even as Lake was writing, however, this situation was changing.

In the 1970s, Congress became more interested in Africa, but in an episodic and inconsistent way. On some issues—especially UN sanctions against a rebellious white government in southern Rhodesia—conservatives, mostly Southern democrats such as Senator Byrd of Virginia, played a decisive role. On other issues—especially those involving development assistance policy and intervention in the Angolan civil war—liberals challenged administration policy. In almost all cases, Congress reacted to presidential moves. Instead of putting issues on the agenda or developing new initiatives, congressmen concentrated on blocking or limiting executive branch action on issues that were already on the agenda.

In the 1980s, Congress began to take the lead in shaping policy toward a number of African issues. More and more, it began to set the agenda and dictate strategies. Three developments—the emergence of a new breed of congressional activists, the expansion of the institutional resources of the U.S. Congress, and a revolution in media coverage of foreign affairs—set the stage for this change.

The rise of foreign policy activism in Congress occurred in the early 1970s. The Vietnam war shattered the old bipartisan consensus that had generally observed the foreign policy Establishment's rule that "politics should stop at the water's edge."[8] Then the Watergate scandal led to the election in 1974 of a large class of young policy "entrepreneurs," mostly liberal Democrats, willing—in fact, eager—to challenge the prerogatives of both the president and their congressional elders.[9] Stephen Solarz, a brash, ambitious, bright, and energetic congressman from New York City, who in 1979 became chairman of the Africa subcommittee of the House Foreign Affairs Committee, typified this new wave. Specializing in foreign policy issues became an accepted way for junior representatives to capture media time and public attention.

The first wave of congressional foreign policy activists were generally liberal. By the late 1970s, however, and especially after the so-called Reagan revolution of the early 1980s, conservative activists such as Newt Gingrich also gained visibility and influence. They banded together to form their own cliques in Congress, such as the "conservative opportunity society." One of the conservatives' priorities was to institutionalize the Reagan doctrine, which called for military assistance to guerrilla movements fighting against pro-Soviet regimes in the Third World.

An increase in the numbers and influence of black congressional representatives paralleled the rise of congressional activism. As table 6.1 shows, their numbers rose slowly but steadily in the 1970s and 1980s. Just as important, as individual black members gained seniority, they were able to accumulate considerable power and institutional clout. By the late 1980s, for example, Congressman William Gray of Pennsylvania had become one of the most influential Democratic party leaders on Capitol Hill.

This development proved especially significant for U.S. policy toward Africa. In 1969, Congressman Charles Diggs became chairman of the House Foreign Affairs Committee's Africa Subcommittee. At first Diggs worked largely on his own to pressure and cajole the Nixon administration on African issues. As the number of black representatives in Congress increased and the Congressional Black Caucus (formed in 1970) began to focus more and more on African issues, Diggs gained allies. By the late 1970s, the caucus had become a dominant force in congressional debates over Africa.

Two institutional developments further enhanced the ability of congressional activists to interject themselves into the foreign policymaking process. The first, and possibly more important, was the growth of congressional staffs. Between 1957 and 1976, the number of staff employees in the House of Representatives increased from 2,441 to 6,939, while the number of staff employees in the Senate increased from 1,115 to 3,251. Informal groupings of members of Congress organized around common bonds and interests or specific issues also proliferated. These groups, usually calling themselves caucuses or task forces, had a variety of objectives—from educating members to coordinating legislative strategies. Among the groups that have had a direct impact on U.S. policy toward Africa are the Congressional Black Caucus, the Congressional Human Rights Caucus, the Congressional Ad Hoc Monitoring Group on Southern Africa, and the Angolan Task Force.

TABLE 6.1. BLACK MEMBERS OF CONGRESS

1970	1971	1973	1975	1977	1981	1983	1985	1987	1991
10	14	16	18	17	18	21	20	23	25

Source: Congressional Black Caucus.

A final factor influencing congressional involvement in African issues was the emergence, as media guru Marshall McLuhan predicted, of a global communications village. When starving Biafran babies, victims of the Nigerian civil war, appeared on our television sets in the late 1960s, the American public for the first time began to witness the human side of Africa's crises. Roger Morris, former White House staff assistant for Africa, provided a graphic example of the impact of this development on presidential actions when he reported how Lyndon Johnson, having seen a television report on the Biafran famine in 1967, crudely instructed State Department officials to send relief in order to "get those nigger babies off my TV set."[10]

Over the past two decades, there have been many "Biafras"—extensively covered human tragedies in Africa. Their increased visibility is due partly to the media's increased ability to cover such stories and partly to the emergence of a network of relief organizations working to get such stories publicized. Greater media coverage has made the American public more sensitive to African crises. And as a result, Congress—the branch of government quickest to react to public concerns—has put more African humanitarian issues on the foreign policy agenda.

The media revolution has also enhanced the influence of congressional activists. Between 1960 and 1976, for example, the number of reporters accredited to Congress increased by 175 percent.[11] The creation of news shows featuring guest interviews, such as the *MacNeil–Lehrer NewsHour* and ABC's *Nightline,* expanded the opportunities for articulate, informed members of Congress to publicize their views. Cable television has further increased exposure, especially with C–SPAN's live broadcasts of important hearings and floor debates. A study showing that members elected in 1978 were three times more likely to use the congressional recording studio than members elected in 1958 demonstrated the growing media consciousness of newer members of Congress.[12]

Congressional activism coupled with a broader public constituency have had a significant impact on policy toward Africa. Among recent developments are:

- An extensive U.S. relief effort in the Horn of Africa that is closely monitored by the House Select Committee on Hunger;

- A series of sanctions, including the Comprehensive Anti-Apartheid Act of 1986, to pressure the South African government to end apartheid;

- Legislation and other action—beginning with the 1985 repeal of the Clark amendment, which had barred aid to Angolan groups—to promote covert military assistance to UNITA rebels;

- Limits on assistance to African countries because of persistent patterns of human rights abuse;

- Requirements that U.S. aid promote the role of women in development, environmental protection, and popular participation in government elections.

The growing role of Congress in foreign policy increases the ability of domestic constituencies concerned with Africa to influence policy. Members of Congress can derive significant political benefits (and campaign contributions) from associating themselves with powerful constituencies and by championing attractive causes such as humanitarian relief, human rights, and environmental protection. This domestic political reality gives representatives of these constituencies far better access to Congress than they can ever hope to have to the foreign policy bureaucracy.

But there is a potential downside to congressional activism. While members of Congress have a clear interest in appearing to be on the "right" side of an issue, it usually does not make much difference to them whether or not their actions produce real results. As long as they are on record as opposing apartheid, hunger, and dictatorship, few need to worry that apartheid, hunger, and dictatorships persist. For these reasons, Congress is often long on symbolism and short on substance.

The dangers inherent in this situation are evident in the current debate surrounding U.S. foreign assistance levels.[13] In 1990, the Congressional Black Caucus succeeded in raising the level of aid to Africa from $560 million to $800 million, and there is a good chance that they will increase that total to $1 billion. This success is widely perceived as a significant victory for Africa. But there is little reason to believe that more aid will substantially improve economic and political conditions on the continent. In fact, more of the same kinds of assistance that have been provided in the past may do more harm than good. (See Chapter 10.)

If congressional activism is to produce lasting benefits for Africa and the United States, two steps must be taken. First, a strategy must be developed to inform and direct that activism; and second, U.S. domestic constituencies must require their elected officials to produce results, not just rhetoric and votes.

7

CHANGING INTERNATIONAL REALITIES

U.S. policy toward Africa in the 1990s and beyond will be shaped by the nature of the post–Cold War international system and the role the United States ultimately assumes in that system. American perceptions of the global significance of events in Africa have largely determined the extent of Washington's interest in the continent—and hence its desire and willingness to be involved there. And they are likely to continue to do so. Moreover, the standing of the United States in the international system—how much and what kinds of power it possesses in relation to other global powers—will significantly affect its ability to play a role. Each of these points requires more detailed examination.

THE GLOBAL NATURE OF AMERICAN INTEREST IN AFRICA

Global considerations carry more weight in the formulation of U.S. policy toward Africa than toward other continents, countries, or regions where the United States has greater intrinsic interests. It is a safe bet that senior officials in Washington will continue to believe that under almost any circumstances, the United States has critical interests in Canada, Mexico, Japan, Great Britain, Germany, and France, and in regions such as Western Europe, northeast Asia, and the Persian Gulf. That is not true for any sub-Saharan African country or region.*

* The only country in sub-Saharan Africa where the United States has substantial bilateral interests is South Africa. American interests in South Africa derive, first, from the strong ties that have developed between significant sectors of American society (especially black society) and South African society and, second, from the fact that it is the only African country with the potential to become a significant industrial power in the early decades of the twenty-first century. Even in South Africa, however, global considerations are likely to be much more important than bilateral ones in determining how much attention it will receive from senior officials. For example, the end of the Cold War significantly reduced Washington's anxiety about and hence interest in developments there. The United States also has important bilateral economic interests in a few other

54

With the collapse of the Soviet challenge in Africa, conta.
ing communism no longer provides policymakers with a fram
work for deciding which African events are important. Th_
future of U.S. policy toward Africa will be influenced decisively
by whatever framework replaces containment.

In the brief period since the dawn of the post–Cold War era,
five alternatives have received the most attention.

"Controlling Third World Instability"

U.S. defense planners were quick to realize the challenge to their
institutional interests posed by the decreasing salience of containment. As a result, they have spent considerable time elaborating a
new rationale for U.S. involvement in the Third World. In early
1990, Secretary of Defense Richard Cheney, chairman of the Joint
Chiefs of Staff General Colin Powell, and the heads of all branches
of the armed services echoed each other in congressional testimony
defending the Pentagon's 1991 budget requests. Their common
theme was that the end of the Cold War will increase instability in
the Third World, which could, in turn, threaten U.S. global interests. During one hearing, General Powell declared that "In this
period of remarkable world change and its attendant instability, it is
important that we and our allies continue to provide an overarch-
ing framework of stability."[1] Arguing against cuts in the U.S. security assistance program, Secretary Cheney testified in February
1990 that "Even if Soviet-sponsored threats to our friends in [the
Middle East] and other [regions] diminish, our friends and allies
will continue to face the prospect of regional, ethnic, and economic conflict. Security assistance will be all the more necessary
to help them in the face of overt aggression or in their attempts to
cope with low intensity conflict."[2] One year later, he testified:

> The gulf crisis has illustrated once again that these regional crises
> and conflicts are likely to arise or to escalate unpredictably and on
> very short notice. This will require that we be able to respond if
> necessary, very rapidly, often very far from home and against
> hostile forces that are increasingly well-armed with conventional
> and unconventional capabilities.[3]

African countries—expecially Angola and Nigeria—but they are not substantial when
compared with U.S. interests in other countries around the world. (See tables 9.2 and
10.1.)

So far, this concern about Third World instability has not caused senior administration officials to focus much attention on Africa. In fact, neither Secretary Cheney nor General Powell normally mentions Africa in speeches or congressional testimony. Nor has the Bush administration expressed much alarm about threats to U.S. interests arising from the conflicts in Ethiopia, Liberia, Mozambique, Rwanda, Somalia, and Sudan. Over time, however, it is inevitable that American officials and interest groups that have an interest in an expanded U.S. presence on the continent (and those African political and military leaders who have depended on U.S. aid for their survival) will attempt to use the specter of instability to rationalize intervention. In this regard, it is important to note that the U.S. military has already begun to expand its special operations capabilities for Africa. In fact, there are plans to activate a Special Forces Group that will be oriented toward the continent.[4]

"Collective Security"

A related theme that could justify a global American military presence in the post–Cold War era is collective security. Support for collective security derives from a belief that America's refusal to join the League of Nations and its failure to respond when Germany, Italy, and Japan first launched attacks against weak states in the 1930s led to World War II. Throughout the Cold War, collective security was often invoked to justify U.S. actions that were motivated principally by the U.S. commitment to containment. With the end of the Cold War, some opinion leaders argue that the United States should make collective security a cardinal principle of American foreign policy.

During the Persian Gulf crisis, President Bush strongly endorsed this view. "We're in the Gulf," he declared in November 1990, "because the world must not and cannot reward aggression."[5] In a speech to the UN General Assembly, the president explained that "not since 1945 have we seen the real possibility of using the United Nations as it was designed—as a center for international collective security."[6] A global commitment to guarantee collective security would impose a special burden on the United States because, in President Bush's words, "We are the only nation on this earth that could assemble the forces of peace."[7]

Many commentators have questioned the sincerity of the administration's commitment to the principle of collective security. But even if it is genuine, there are good reasons to doubt that Africa will be affected. Few if any of the continent's recent wars have involved classical cases of aggression where one state invades another. Rather, they are mostly civil wars, where external intervention usually consists of indirect and often unacknowledged aid to one of the warring parties. In addition, there are no African Iraqs—that is, strong regional military powers poised to invade neighboring states. Even Libya, which was perceived in such terms by the Reagan administration, no longer excites much fear in Washington.

"Promoting Democracy"

A theme that is likely to affect U.S. policy toward Africa is "promoting democracy." In February 1990, Secretary of State James Baker testified before Congress that "our first and preeminent challenge is consolidating democracy."[8] The secretary reiterated this position during the July 1990 Economic Summit in Houston when he declared that "the summit partners share the imperative of our time: to help promote and to help secure democracy around the world."[9]

Support for placing spread-of-democracy initiatives at the top of the U.S. foreign policy agenda increased markedly during the 1980s. President Reagan initially embraced this theme as a means of winning support for anti-Communist guerrillas in Afghanistan and Nicaragua. But it quickly gained a momentum of its own, appealing especially to neoconservatives. For example, columnist Ben Wattenberg, one of the most outspoken advocates of a campaign to export American-style democracy, declared in March 1989: "It is time for a new bumper sticker. . . . Americans have a missionary streak, and democracy is our mission. The new sticker should read 'pro-democracy.' "[10] Six months later, he wrote: "The Cold War is probably ending.

Let's not only end it, but win it. Play offense, America. Extend democracy."[11]

Promoting democracy has been a recurring theme of American diplomacy at least since the days of Woodrow Wilson. What makes the current era different is that a growing segment of the foreign policy Establishment believes both that the global triumph of liberal democratic ideals is now inevitable[12] and that the United States has the power and freedom to make the promotion of democracy its first priority.[13] The number of American opinion leaders who believe that promoting democracy is a "very important" foreign policy goal is growing. According to one survey, the percentage who hold this belief has risen steadily from 7 percent in 1976, to 10 percent in 1980 and 18 percent in 1984, to 24 percent in 1988.[14] A 1990 survey found that 26 percent of American leaders (and 28 percent of the public) felt it was very important that the United States help "to bring a democratic form of government to other nations."[15] This is not yet a large and committed constituency, but the foreign policy bureaucracy has already begun to exploit political interest in promoting democracy. In December 1990, the U.S. Agency for International Development (AID) announced "The Democracy Initiative," a program "to help promote and consolidate democracy as the legitimate organizing principle for political systems throughout the world."[16]

In the few public speeches he has given since taking office, the Bush administration's chief Africanist, Assistant Secretary of State Cohen, has emphasized the need to encourage democracy in Africa. In November 1990, he declared that "the United States is heartened by the democratic trend in Africa," and announced that "we intend to pay special attention to Africa's democracies and to countries that are actively engaged in the democratization process."[17] Both AID and the State Department's Africa bureau will use the need to encourage democratization as a rationale for maintaining aid levels and expanding their presence on the continent.* For example, in his November 1990 speech, Cohen

---

* AID has embraced the democracy theme in a much more thoughtful, deliberate, and (in my judgment) sincere manner than the State Department's Africa bureau. See U.S. Agency for International Development, *The Democracy Initiative* (Washington, D.C., December 1990).

spoke of "exploring the possibility of obtaining new types of funding which we could use to help those countries which are pursuing the interlinked and mutually reinforcing goals of political liberalization and market-oriented economic reform."[18]

Unfortunately, America's enthusiasm for promoting democracy can be manipulated easily so as to rationalize the maintenance of ties with a variety of unsavory African leaders. An illustration of this was seen in an October 1990 speech in Washington by Angolan guerrilla leader Jonas Savimbi. "I can tell you today," he informed his audience,

> Americans have no further reason for cynicism about the possibilities for democracy in Africa. The verdict has been rendered in the many experiments in government that have been tried in Africa. Most people in Africa, including those of us in UNITA, have learned a great deal about the direction in which we should take our countries. We know that political development must coincide with economic development. So I don't ask you to support UNITA as a political party, but rather to support and encourage, as you have done in Eastern Europe, Latin America and Asia, a political process which will culminate in a democratic Angola.[19]

It is instructive that Savimbi, whose well-paid Washington publicists have kept a close watch over the changing American mood, spoke at length about democracy while making almost no mention of the theme he emphasized most frequently in similar speeches delivered in the 1980s—the dangers and evils of the Soviet presence in Angola.

"North-South Interdependence"

Among American liberals, there is considerable support for the idea that U.S. foreign policy should reflect the growing interdependence between the welfare of the Third World and the welfare of advanced industrial countries. For example, the writer Richard Barnet has argued that

> the United States is organically connected to societies across the planet which are in a position to export considerable misery to our shores. . . . The effects of the worldwide boom in the narcotics industry, the spread of ozone-depleting agriculture, and the public-health crises in distant, poor countries cannot be kept from American shores by military means or, it seems, by any other—

except the building of stable economies and a more equitable social
order within those countries.[20]

Other analysts, such as John Sewell of the Overseas Development Council, emphasize the potentially positive link between economic growth in developing countries and the revitalization of the U.S. economy. In Sewell's words, "Sustained and rapid economic growth in the Third World, particularly in the middle-income developing countries, is now of direct importance to the United States because it could be a key element in making significant progress toward reducing the U.S. trade deficit without inducing a global recession."[21]

In addition to such practical interests, advocates of increased aid to Africa argue that we have a moral responsibility to address the problems of developing countries. This view was clearly reflected in the 1986 report of the Committee on African Development Strategies that was jointly sponsored by the Council on Foreign Relations and the Overseas Development Council. The Committee's "Compact for African Development" declared "As a political, economic and technological world power, and as a nation with a history of deep commitments to helping those who help themselves, the United States has a unique potential and responsibility to work with the people and governments of Africa."[22]

Similar themes have been used to defend U.S. development assistance to Africa since the late 1950s. But it is not clear that they have a strong public appeal. Some studies indicate considerable support for assisting developing countries, but others are more ambivalent. For example, the Chicago Council on Foreign Relations recently found that 41 percent of the American public and 42 percent of American "leaders" believed that "helping to improve the standard of living of less developed nations" was a "very important" foreign policy goal.[23] But the same survey also showed that only 23 percent of the public, as opposed to 54 percent of the leaders, were in favor of increased economic aid to the underdeveloped nations of Africa and Asia.[24] Moreover, one factor that accounts for public ambivalence about foreign assistance is the widespread perception that aid monies are misused by foreign governments and wasted by the U.S. bureaucracy.[25]

"Nonintervention and Neoisolation"

A growing number of foreign policy analysts reject all four of the preceding rationales for continued involvement and intervention in the Third World. Instead, they argue that the United States should abandon its post–World War II internationalist policies in favor of a much less interventionist strategy. For example, conservative columnist Patrick Buchanan advocates a policy of "enlightened nationalism," a term borrowed from Walter Lippmann. He urges Americans to "look . . . with a cold eye on the international set, [who are] never at a loss for new ideas to divert U.S. wealth and power into crusades and causes having little or nothing to do with the true national interest of the United States."[26] Buchanan is not alone in calling for an end to global interventionism.

A growing school of so-called neo-Realists oppose U.S. intervention in the Third World. Following the logic of George Kennan, Lippmann, and leading academic "realists" of the postwar era such as Hans Morgenthau and Kenneth Waltz, these analysts argue that U.S. interests in most of the Third World are neither substantial nor threatened. They question Washington's need to worry about instability and aggression in Africa and doubt the ability of the United States to promote democracy. In one of the clearest statements of this position, Professor Stephen Van Evera has recommended that

> the United States should cease intervening to "protect national security" or to "bolster Third World democracy," since the results of intervention seldom serve either purpose. And the United States should never use force on a large scale in the Third World, because the U.S. has no Third World interest that can justify paying large costs or taking large numbers of lives.[27]

It is possible that the foreign policy Establishment will not unite around any of these themes. The world may be too complex, threats to U.S. interests too diffuse, and American politics too fragmented for the creation of a new consensus. Without a unifying theme, U.S. policy toward Africa could become the focus of an intense and unending struggle among competing camps in the foreign policy community, each seeking to impose its own global agenda on the continent. This could create the worst of all possible situations: an incoherent mix of inaction, haphazard involvement, and quixotic intervention that neither serves American interests nor benefits the continent.

THE CHANGING NATURE OF U.S. GLOBAL POWER

The ability of the United States to influence developments in Africa has always derived from its power and standing in the international system. The difference between U.S. influence in Africa and its influence in Latin America illustrates the point: the United States was a superpower in the Western Hemisphere long before it became a global superpower, and it is likely to remain a superpower in this hemisphere even if it loses its global status. The reasons are obvious. First, the country's physical presence in North America means that its shadow will be cast across the hemisphere automatically and effortlessly. In fact, the United States cannot choose not to affect its neighbors—economically, politically, and culturally. Second, the status of the United States in the region is based, primarily, on the discrepancy between U.S. power and the power of other states in the hemisphere. A decline in U.S. power vis-à-vis other global powers would not necessarily change the hemispheric balance of power. Neither of these conditions applies in Africa.

The United States is not an immediate and constant force in Africa, as it is in the Americas. Europe and the Middle East are much more a part of the African landscape than is the United States. Americans can (and more often than not do) choose not to get involved in Africa. U.S. influence, therefore, derives more from its power relative to other global powers (for example, China, France, Great Britain, Japan, and the Soviet Union) than from the overwhelming discrepancy between U.S. capabilities and those of African states. If the relative power of the United States declines, U.S. influence in Africa will decline. For these reasons, the ongoing debate over "the decline" of American power matters greatly to Africa.

8

THE LIMITS OF U.S. ECONOMIC POWER IN AFRICA

Over the past three decades, Americans concerned about dismal economic conditions in Africa have often called for an African equivalent of the Marshall Plan—the massive U.S. economic aid program that was created in the late 1940s to help rebuild Western Europe. It would be a mistake, however, to expect such appeals to ever be answered. The United States could do a lot more to help Africans than it is currently doing. But treating a comprehensive American aid package as the solution to Africa's problems makes no sense. Even at the height of its global economic dominance, the United States did not possess the knowledge, resources, or will necessary to deliver such a package. Today its capabilities are even more limited.

By the late 1960s, the relative economic power of the United States had declined substantially.[1] In the years immediately following World War II, the United States accounted for roughly one-third to two-fifths of the total global product; by the mid-1960s, it accounted for slightly less than one-quarter. As Joseph Nye has argued, much of this decline was an inevitable result of the fading of "the World War Two effect."[2] But he is wrong to suggest that because this decline was to be expected, it has not caused a fundamental change in the ability of the United States to exercise global leadership. In early 1990, Senator David Boren, chairman of the Select Committee on Intelligence, explained, "Economically, the allies no longer need the U.S. the way they did in 1950, when we had two-thirds of the world's assets and nine of the ten largest banks in the world."[3] After observing the July 1990 economic summit in Houston, journalist R. W. Apple wrote: "Once upon a time, the United States was able, within the bounds of good sense and good taste, to get what it wanted at the annual meetings of the seven strongest industrial nations. At this week's meeting . . . that was manifestly no longer true. It will probably not be true again any time soon."[4]

The fact is that the United States was never the predominant economic force in Africa. Throughout the early postwar era, for example, the United States seldom accounted for more than 10 percent of total trade with Africa. In contrast, Europe accounted for well over half of Africa's trade with the world. (See table 8.1.)

Aid figures provide another, and for Africa even more telling, indicator of the declining economic power of the United States. Once among the most generous aid donors, the United States now contributes a smaller proportion of gross national product (GNP) to overseas development assistance (ODA) than any other major economic power. (See table 8.2.) As a result, the U.S. share of total world ODA has shrunk considerably. (See table 8.3.)

TABLE 8.1. U.S. SHARE OF WORLD TRADE WITH AFRICA, 1938–1970
(Percent of World Total)

	1938	1948	1960	1970	1980	1985	1988
U.S. Exports to Africa	9	18	10	11	9	10	7
U.S. Imports from Africa	4	7	7	10	27	19	18

Source: International Monetary Fund, *Direction of Trade* (Washington D.C.: International Monetary Fund, miscellaneous years).

TABLE 8.2. ODA AS PERCENTAGE OF GNP

	1965	1975	1985	1988–1989
U.S.	0.58	0.27	0.24	0.18
Japan	0.27	0.23	0.29	0.32
Germany	0.40	0.40	0.47	0.40
France	0.76	0.62	0.78	0.75
Italy	0.10	0.11	0.26	0.40
U.K.	0.47	0.39	0.33	0.32

Source: Development Assistance Committee, *Development Cooperation* (Paris: OECD, various years).

TABLE 8.3. SHARE OF WORLD ODA

	1970–1971	1975–1976	1980–1981	1988–1989
U.S.	25%	17%	16%	16%
Europe	34%	28%	31%	40%
Japan	9%	7%	11%	17%

Source: Development Assistance Committee, *Development Cooperation* (Paris: OECD, various years).

France, Germany, and Japan give Africa a considerably greater proportion of the total development assistance funds than does the United States. (See figures 8.1 and 8.2.)

Given these economic realities, it is wrong to assume (as is often done in debates concerning U.S. policy toward Africa) that

FIGURE 8.1. AID TO AFRICA, 1989
DISTRIBUTION BY DONOR

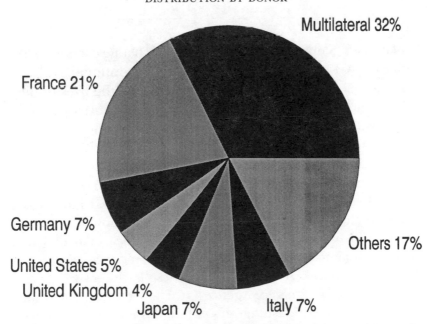

Source: OECD, *Development Cooperation, 1990 Report* (Paris: OECD, December 1990).

FIGURE 8.2. AID TO AFRICA, 1989
SHARE OF DONOR'S TOTAL AID CONTRIBUTION

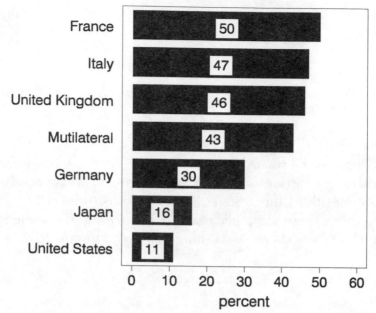

Source: OECD, *Development Cooperation, 1990 Report* (Paris: OECD, December 1990).

unilateral U.S. measures will significantly change economic conditions in Africa. Whatever the outcome of the annual battles on Capitol Hill over aid allocations, the effect on the lives of most Africans is not likely to be significant. Similarly, attempts to use unilateral economic sanctions to influence the political behavior of African governments is not likely to have much effect.

On the other hand, the decline in the relative economic position of the United States has not (so far) translated into diminished U.S. influence in multilateral economic institutions. In most cases, therefore, how Washington uses its power within multilateral institutions will have a far greater impact on Africa than unilateral actions, as almost one-third of the development assistance that flows to the continent flows through these institutions.

Although Japan's emergence as the world's leading creditor nation has eroded Washington's nominal power within international financial institutions, the United States is still the most powerful actor in the multilateral board rooms. One reason for this is because of what Shafiqul Islam, an economist at the Council on Foreign Relations, has described as the "burden-power gap" that exists on the governing bodies of these institutions. Shortages of trained Japanese economists and deliberate actions by the United States and the leading European economic powers have prevented Japan from exercising as much influence as its financial contributions would otherwise allow.[5] This situation will change as Japan becomes more self-confident and assertive as a global economic power; at that time, U.S. multilateral economic clout is likely to decline in much the same way that the influence of unilateral U.S. actions has declined.

In short, the United States is not now and never has been the most decisive economic actor in Africa. Acting alone, Washington cannot significantly affect economic developments and trends on the continent. By itself, it can do little to boost Africa's trade prospects, reform its economies, or resolve its debt problems. All of these issues must be dealt with multilaterally through international institutions such as the International Monetary Fund (IMF), the World Bank, and the many specialized agencies of the United Nations.*

* A strategy to make more effective use of the United States' limited economic influence in Africa is developed in Herbst, *U.S. Economic Policy Toward Africa in the 1990s* (New York: Council on Foreign Relations Press, forthcoming).

9

THE GLOBAL REACH OF AMERICAN SOCIETY

Of all the global sea changes that are currently unfolding, the one that could most affect the ways in which the United States relates to Africa in the twenty-first century is the emergence of a truly transnational society. Transnational society consists of non-official, nongovernmental interactions and exchanges that occur among individuals and groups across national boundaries. It is a jumble of actors and activities encompassing business partnerships, professional associations, cultural exchanges, educational links, ethnic ties, and religious bonds. Two traits above all else characterize transnational society: it is separate from, albeit not entirely independent of, governments; and it is highly pluralistic. As a transnational society develops, bringing more and more Americans into contact with more and more Africans, American influence will increase, but the power and independence of U.S. officials will shrink.

Throughout the history of the modern world, the most significant actors in the international system have been nation-states. Events have usually confounded those who heralded the dawn of a new age in which relations among peoples would supplant relations among states. Nonetheless, there are compelling reasons for believing that a quantum expansion of transnational society is currently underway.

THE EXPANSION OF TRANSNATIONAL SOCIETY

The accelerating expansion of transnational society is a result of several forces. Among the most important of these is the modern transportation-communication-information revolution that has occurred over the past century. People, products, information, and ideas now move across the globe more easily and rapidly than even the most prophetic scientists and strategists could have imagined.

The growing accessibility and declining cost of electro¡
nication via computers and fax machines has made it i¡
easier for individuals and groups to communicate daily. '
opment of global television networks (which is inevita¡
wake of the Cable News Network's pioneering efforts to g ⌐.ⁱ ᴜᴉe
air around the world) will further shrink the world.

Another indicator of the expansion of transnational society
is the proliferation of international nongovernmental organizations (NGOs). These organizations play an important role in
bringing together individuals with similar interests from different countries, and hence multiplying people-to-people contacts.
Since the end of World War II, the number of international
NGOs has increased markedly. (See figure 9.1.) Participation is

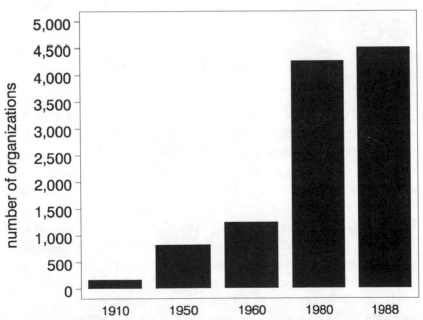

FIGURE 9.1. GROWTH OF INTERNATIONAL NONGOVERNMENTAL
ORGANIZATIONS
1910 TO 1988

Source: Union of International Associations, *International Organization Participation 1988/89* (New York: K. G. Saur, June 1988).

greatest among citizens of industrial countries, but Third World representation is rapidly increasing. In part, this is the result of an explosion of activity at the grass-roots level in many Third World countries. According to Alan Durning of World Watch, "A lattice-work of nongovernmental organizations is spreading across continents with organizations in one country sharing fundamental characteristics with organizations in another. . . . Community activism in the Third World is bringing new actors to international affairs."[1]

The collapse of communism in Eastern Europe will greatly accelerate the expansion of transnational society. Although some Communist regimes failed to prevent the emergence of an oppositional civil society within their boundaries, others (Bulgaria, East Germany, and Romania) succeeded in smothering independent associational life. Almost all controlled the freedom of individuals and groups to establish links with other societies. The demise of totalitarian rule has thus removed an important limit on the growth of society-to-society linkages. Today, with the possible exception of China, no state anywhere in the world is both committed to and capable of resisting the attractions of transnational society.

THE GLOBAL INFLUENCE OF AMERICAN CIVIL SOCIETY

The United States has become, in Ben Wattenberg's words, "the most culturally potent nation in the world."[2] Among the indicators Wattenberg uses to prove this point are the following: sixty countries received the 1990 Super Bowl broadcast; ninety countries now receive CNN signals; the volume of sales of American television programming to foreign broadcasters now exceeds $2 billion annually. Wattenberg actually fails to mention one of America's most powerful cultural resources, rock music. International relations theorists may scoff at the idea that such trends deserve to be discussed in the same breath with nuclear weapons and trade balances, but not American businessmen. As a December 1991 cover story in *Fortune* magazine noted, pop culture (rock music, television programs, movies) has become one of the most important foreign exchange earners for the United States[3] and an increasingly significant force in international politics. "Pop foreign policy" has had a significant influence on American attitudes toward a number of international issues—including famine relief in Ethiopia (1985 Live Aid concert), apartheid (1987 "Ain't Gonna Play Sun City" song and video), human rights (1989 world concert tour organized by Amnesty International), rain forest preservation, and, in an earlier era, the Vietnam war. As more and more American celebrities take up international causes, the importance of pop foreign policy will grow, especially for regions such as Africa where changing public moods so strongly determine patterns of international involvement.

Just as important as the globalization of American pop culture is the transnational reach of American civil society. As Alexis de Tocqueville observed in the early nineteenth century, American society differs from others in the richness of associational activity. In *Democracy in America,* he wrote:

> In no other country in the world has the principle of association been more successfully used, or applied to a greater multitude of objects, than in America. Besides the permanent associations, which are established by law, under the names of townships, cities, and counties, a vast number of others are formed and maintained by the agency of private individuals.[4]

More recently, social theorist Peter Drucker has noted that "American society has become different and distinct from other countries—developed or developing, free market or socialist—in the steady growth of its third sector, the thousands of nonprofit but non-governmental institutions."[5] He calls the nonprofit sector the "fastest growing part of American society"[6] in the 1980s. Nowhere else in the world can be found such a dizzying array of churches, trade unions, professional associations, civic organizations, and the like. In 1989, the *World Almanac* listed 21,911 *national* nonprofit associations alone. The number of local groups across the country is incalculable. According to one estimate, the "yearly budget of the American nonprofit sector exceeds the budget of all but seven nations in the world."[7]

Although few reliable statistics are available, the overseas activities of these groups have increased visibly in recent years. According to one report the number of private voluntary organizations registered with the U.S. Agency for International Development tripled between 1973 and 1989.[8] A 1984 study by the Council on Foundations revealed that half of the 485 U.S. national religious organizations had operations internationally.[9] In *Bridging the Global Gap: A Handbook to Linking Citizens of the First and Third Worlds,* Medea Benjamin and Andrea Freedman list over two hundred American-based organizations actively involved with Third World issues and peoples.[10] The range of groups they list is amazingly heterogeneous, politically as well as professionally. It includes the following:

- Habitat for Humanity, a Christian housing ministry that builds houses in twenty countries around the world;

- International Sister Restaurant Project, a technical assistance program organized by the owner of a Philadelphia café;

- U.S.–South Africa Sister Community Project, a San Francisco–based group linking U.S. cities with black communities in South Africa;

- Grassroots International, a project that supports grassroots development in the Horn of Africa, Lebanon, the Philippines, and South Africa;

- International Voluntary Service, which provides technical assistance volunteers to small-scale rural development projects;

- Plenty USA, a Tennessee-based group that sends volunteers to work on community development in Central America and Africa;

- World Neighbors, an Oklahoma-based organization that promotes small-scale, locally controlled, and technologically appropriate agricultural systems;

- International Design Assistance Commission, a loose federation of volunteer designers who assist international agencies with Third World projects;

- Physicians for Human Rights, an organization that enlists health workers in human rights work;

- Vosh International, a Missouri-based group of optometrists dedicated to improving the vision of disadvantaged people around the world;

- Women's World Banking, an organization that guarantees loans to women entrepreneurs around the world.

The largest and most comprehensive program to develop bonds between Americans and peoples abroad is the sister cities program. Started in the late 1950s at the urging of President Eisenhower, this program has fostered ties between over eight hundred American cities and roughly fifteen hundred cities overseas. (See table 9.1.)

In addition, individual U.S. states and localities are interjecting themselves into international relations in a host of ways. According to Michael Shuman of the Center for Innovative Diplomacy, "more than 1,000 U.S. state and local governments of all political stripes are participating in foreign affairs and their numbers are expanding daily."[11] They are doing so in a myriad of ways, including passing laws restricting companies from doing business with South Africa, providing sanctuary for refugees from central America, establishing local nuclear free zones, and creating their own international investment offices.

TABLE 9.1. GEOGRAPHIC DISTRIBUTION OF U.S. SISTER CITIES

Region	Number of U.S. Cities
Africa	65
Americas/Caribbean	310
Europe	525
Asia/Oceania	410
Middle East	33

Source: Sister Cities International, *Directory of Sister Cities, Counties and States by State and County* (Alexandria, Virginia: Sister Cities International, 1990).

Americans also tend to organize and contribute to charities much more than citizens of other industrialized nations. Brian and Ann Brown O'Connell of the Foundation Center have observed that "the United States is the only country in the world where giving and volunteering are pervasive characteristics of the total society."[12] This charitable impulse has manifested itself in several ways. The relief efforts of groups listed earlier in table 5.1 are sustained largely by private donations. But the most important philanthropic influence on U.S. relations with the world at large has been the expanding community of private foundations.

In 1990, U.S. private foundations had a total asset base of roughly $125 billion. In that year, foundations collectively gave out more than $7 billion in grants. Although still a small proportion of total grants (11 percent in 1987), the amount of money committed to international projects is increasing.[13] The larger foundations—such as the Ford Foundation, the Rockefeller Foundation, the Carnegie Corporation of New York, and the John T. and Catherine MacArthur Foundation—influence U.S. relations with the world in a number of ways. Very few of the major U.S. organizations concerned with international relations could survive without foundation support of one kind or another; this is especially true of organizations focused on regions such as Africa that are not of interest to most major individual or corporate benefactors. On some issues—most notably South Africa—U.S. foundations have sought to encourage and shape policy debates by sponsoring highly visible policy commissions. Increasingly, they have started to play a more active foreign policy role by directly assisting private individuals and groups overseas working for economic and political change.

The global reach of America's private sector is expanding rapidly. As important as the revolution in communications technology is the increasingly common use of English as an international language. In 1988, the British political economist Susan Strange wrote that "the American language has become the lingua franca of the global economy and of transnational social and professional groups. . . . American universities [have] come to dominate learning and the major professions not only because

TABLE 9.2.   ORIGINS OF NEW IMMIGRANTS TO THE UNITED STATES
(Percentage distribution)

	1820–1988	1961–1970	1971–1980	1981–1986
Europe	68	34	18	11
Asia	10	13	35	48
Americas	21	52	44	38
Africa	1	1	2	3
Other	<1	1	1	1
Total	100	100	100	100

Source: U.S. Bureau of Immigration and Naturalization.

they have numbers and resources of libraries and finance but also because their work is conducted in English."[14] The numbers documenting this trend are astounding. In 1987, for example, Americans made 4.7 billion minutes of overseas telephone calls, and over 85 percent of all international telephone conversations took place in English. Furthermore, over 80 percent of all the information stored in computers around the world is stored in English.[15]

Interaction between American society and other societies is also facilitated by the ethnic diversity of the U.S. population. As of 1990, roughly 23 percent of the U.S. population was black, Hispanic, or Asian. Immigration and other demographic changes are transforming the United States into an even more racially and ethnically diverse nation. Since 1960, most new American immigrants have come from the Third World. (See table 9.2.)

Private contacts between hyphenated Americans and their homelands are growing by leaps and bounds. Among examples of the diverse ways these contacts are maintained is the fax network that linked Chinese students in the United States with their brethren in China at the time of the Tiananmen Square massacre; the ties that have developed between African-Americans and black South African opposition groups; the economic linkages developing between Asian-Americans and business interests in northeast Asia; and the transborder communities that are being created along the U.S.–Mexico frontier.

10

A DISMAL BALANCE SHEET

The United States has an unprecedented opportunity to re-orient its relations with the African continent. The end of the Cold War has freed U.S. policymakers to explore new ideas and approaches. U.S. military and economic interests in Africa have largely become inconsequential. This should make it possible for the United States to pursue principled, humanitarian policies that will serve the mutual interests of Americans and Africans. But there is no guarantee that U.S. policymakers will use their newfound freedom in creative and positive ways.

If left to their own devices, the bureaucrats and politicians responsible for formulating U.S. policy toward Africa are likely to play the same kinds of diplomatic and political games that they have played in the past. For one thing, new policies—such as those proposed in the final chapter of this book—would reduce their influence over U.S.–African relations. For another, few American officials (or opinion leaders) actually perceive the need for fundamental change. Most of them are convinced that the Soviet Union's retreat from the battlefields of the Third World and the collapse of communism in Eastern Europe have vindicated the old ideas and strategies that informed American foreign policy from 1945 to 1989. This judgment fails to take into account the damage done to African societies by past U.S. policies.

By only one criterion—containing communism—did U.S. policy succeed in Africa; and it is not clear how much credit American officials deserve for that success.* By other important criteria—such as promoting development, encouraging democ-

* The Soviet threat to Africa was never as serious as it was portrayed by most policy-makers. Moscow's greatest successes were made possible by U.S. blunders. In Angola, for example, the Kremlin scored a geopolitical victory in the mid-1970s largely because of decisions by the Johnson and Nixon administrations to subordinate concerns about Portuguese colonialism to a desire to avoid a conflict with Lisbon and the failure of Secretary of State Kissinger to pay attention to events in Angola in 1974–75 until it was

racy, and limiting regional conflict—U.S. efforts in Africa failed dismally. Isolated successes were achieved in facilitating transfers of power from white minorities to black majorities in Zimbabwe (1979–80) and Namibia (1988–90). But these much-celebrated diplomatic triumphs were outweighed by the larger number of unacknowledged failures in Angola, Ethiopia, Liberia, Somalia, Sudan, Zaire, and other countries. One way to assess past policies is to examine the balance sheet for U.S. efforts in those countries where Washington spent the largest sums of American taxpayers' dollars.

From 1962 to 1988, six countries—Ethiopia, Kenya, Liberia, Somalia, Sudan, and Zaire—received the largest share of U.S. assistance to Africa. In all six countries, the bulk of American aid went to one leader. (See table 10.1.)

By any standard, this is not a list of African success stories. Of the six rulers who received the greatest amount of U.S. assistance during the Cold War, only one—Daniel Arap Moi, Kenya—was elected to office. Four of Washington's clients were eventually ousted following a coup or civil war: Haile Selassie II, Ethiopia (September 1974), Gaafar Nimeri, Sudan (April 1985), Samuel Doe, Liberia (September 1990), and Siad Barre, Somalia (January 1991). After receiving substantial U.S. aid, five of these countries—Ethiopia, Liberia, Somalia, Sudan, and Zaire—have experienced bloody civil wars that killed tens of thousands of people. In addition, four of those* had consistently worse economic growth rates than the average for other sub-Saharan African countries; and those same four countries are now literally bankrupt. (See table 10.2.)

Of course, U.S. policy did not by itself cause these disasters; but it did contribute to them in significant ways. The underlying causes of each country's problems were a mix of internal and

---

too late to avoid a no-win confrontation with the Soviet Union. Where Moscow did make gains such as in Ghana, Guinea, and Mali in the early 1960s, Somalia and Sudan in the late 1960s, and Angola, Ethiopia, and Mozambique in the late 1970s, it was not able to sustain them. In the final analysis, U.S. policy did not contain communism. It was contained by the obstinate nature of African realities, the weakness of Moscow's African clients, and the inherent economic and political limits of Soviet power.

* Ethiopia received significant sums of U.S. aid in the mid-1980s but only for famine relief.

TABLE 10.1. U.S. AID TO PRINCIPAL CLIENTS IN AFRICA,
1962 TO 1988

Country	Principal U.S. Client	Aid to Country (total)	Aid to Client	Aid to Client (% of total aid to country)
Ethiopia	Haile Selassie	817	458	56
Kenya	Daniel Arap Moi	1043	652	63
Liberia	Samuel Doe	807	532	66
Somalia	Siad Barre	884	822	93
Sudan	Gaafar Nimeri	1801	1443	80
Zaire	Mobutu Sese Seko	1164	889	76

Source: Agency for International Development, *U.S. Overseas Loans and Grants and Assistance from International Organizations* (Washington, D.C.: Agency for International Development, various years).

TABLE 10.2. ECONOMIC PERFORMANCE OF LEADING RECIPIENTS
OF U.S. AID TO AFRICA

	Average Annual Growth of GNP, 1980–1987 (percent)	Debt as a Percentage of GNP, 1987 (percent)	Gross Foreign Exchange Reserves, 1987 (months of import coverage)
Kenya	−0.9	58	1.4
Liberia	−5.2	108	0.0
Somalia	−2.5	237	0.4
Sudan	−4.3	97	0.1
Zaire	−2.5	140	1.8
Sub-Saharan Africa	−1.2	74	2.0

Source: The World Bank, *Sub-Saharan Africa: From Crisis to Sustainable Growth* (Washington, D.C.: The World Bank, 1989).

external factors unique to each case. In all six countries, however, the proximate cause was the policies of a single ruler. U.S. officials helped those rulers to stay in power by providing them with financial support, military assistance, and political legitimacy. In some cases, Washington encouraged them to pursue misguided strategies. But just as important, American policymakers were often guilty of misleading the American people about the prospects for development and reform and the effects of U.S. involvement in these countries.

In Ethiopia, Kenya, and Somalia, it would be wrong to single out the United States for blame. While U.S. policy did not yield positive returns, Washington was not the principal great power involved. In Kenya, British officials were more influential than their American counterparts. London also aided Haile Selassie, and it helped to create the political mess that is present-day Somalia. But Moscow deserves the largest share of the blame for the tragedies that have befallen Ethiopia and Somalia. In the first half of the 1970s, the Soviets armed Mogadishu (Somalia) to the teeth; then, after Siad Barre used his arsenal to invade Ethiopia in 1977, Moscow switched sides and provided unprecedented amounts of military aid to Addis Ababa. Without Soviet arms, the wars that have raged across the Horn of Africa would have killed far fewer people, and they probably would have ended much earlier.

On the other hand, no other great power is as responsible as the United States for what happened in Liberia, Sudan, and Zaire. Washington readily chose to take the lead in supporting and protecting Doe in Liberia, Nimeri in Sudan, and Mobutu in Zaire. Without U.S. support, Doe and Nimeri would not have survived as long as they did; and Mobutu would not still be in power. Examining these cases together provides a compelling indictment of the way U.S. officials have operated in Africa.

THE UNITED STATES AND MOBUTU

The United States first became involved in Zaire in 1960 when it was a Belgian colony. A precipitate decision by Belgium to grant independence to the Congo, as it was then called, touched off a complicated power struggle in Leopoldville (now Kinshasa) and prompted rebels in the mineral-rich Katanga province to attempt to secede. Fearing that the Soviets might rush into the vacuum created by chaos in the Congo, Washington intervened. First President Eisenhower, and later President Kennedy, approved a variety of covert and overt actions to ensure that pro-Western "moderates" held on to power in Kinshasa. The Kennedy administration also threw its muscle behind a United Nations military operation that helped to end the Katangese secession in January 1963.

During the period leading up to independence, American intelligence officers developed a close relationship with Joseph Mobutu (Mobutu Sese Seko), a Congolese military officer. Mobutu briefly seized power in Kinshasa in September 1960, but then quickly stepped aside in favor of a provisional civilian government. In November 1965, after five years of intermittent civil war and constantly changing governments, he took control for good. Mobutu would not have come to power had it not been for the privileged relationship he had developed with the mid-level CIA officials who exercised considerable influence over U.S. policy toward the Congo in the early 1960s.

Once in power, Mobutu was able to garner and maintain the support of many prominent American diplomats and politicians. U.S. aid to Zaire has flowed at relatively high levels since the 1960s. From 1961 to 1990, no other African country ranked among the top recipients of American aid as consistently as Zaire. But other forms of U.S. support have been even more important to Mobutu's survival.

Three times the United States intervened to help Mobutu quell armed rebellions that threatened his regime. In July 1967, U.S. Air Force C-130 transport planes and 150 airmen helped to dislodge rebels holding key towns in the northeastern part of the country. A decade later the Carter administration (with France, Belgium, and Morocco) came to Mobutu's aid when rebels invaded the Shaba province (formerly Katanga) from Angola in March 1977 and then again in May 1978. Without these interventions, as Nguza Karl-I-Bond, a senior Zairian political figure who has been in and out of exile and government service, told a

U.S. congressional committee, "Mr. Mobutu's regime would not have survived."[1] The United States (along with France and Israel) helped to train and equip the units responsible for ensuring President Mobutu's personal security.

Just as important, U.S. officials have endorsed Mobutu repeatedly in ways that strengthened his domestic and international standing. For example, during a stop in Kinshasa in April 1976 Secretary of State Kissinger spoke of "the respect and affection that lie at the heart of the relationship between" the United States and Zaire; and he assured the Mobutu regime that "the United States will stand by its friends."[2] More recently, President Bush called the Zairian dictator "one of our most valued friends [on] the entire continent of Africa."[3] As a 1990 report by the Lawyers Committee for Human Rights points out, "Mobutu has effectively used [visits by U.S. officials], his meetings with U.S. presidents and other symbolic gestures of support to sustain the perception that the United States condones his conduct, and will stand by his government."[4]

Washington has supported Mobutu despite clear evidence that he has done immense damage to Zaire. Widely regarded as one of the most corrupt rulers in Africa, Mobutu has robbed his country's coffers so thoroughly that he is now one of the world's richest men. A 1982 staff report to the Senate Foreign Relations Committee observed, "If Mobutu's fortune is anywhere near that claimed by both critics and supporters, he could easily replace from his own resources the entire U.S. security assistance program."[5] Yet, over the same period that Mobutu has become so wealthy, the territory he rules has regressed.

Despite tremendous mineral riches and billions of dollars of foreign aid and investment, Zaire was poorer in 1991 than it was at the time of its independence. According to some estimates, the real per-capita income of the average Zairois had shrunk to less than 20 percent of what it was in 1960. Zaire's economic infrastructure has deteriorated, and little has been done to expand its human capital base.

Mobutu has also consistently abused the human rights of Zaire's citizens and prevented the emergence of other centers of power and wealth in the country. In its 1990 report, the Lawyers

Committee for Human Rights concluded that "Zaire's security forces have carried out widespread gross violations of human rights, including political killings, torture and cruel treatment of prisoners, incommunicado detentions and arbitrary arrests and prolonged detentions without trials."[6]

Why has Washington continued to back Mobutu? Over the past three decades, different U.S. officials have given roughly the same answer. In the words of one deputy assistant secretary of state, "Zaire has been a firm friend and has supported U.S. policies; it contributes substantially to stability in central Africa through its pro-Western foreign policy."[7] When asked about U.S. aid to Zaire shortly after taking office, President Jimmy Carter bluntly declared that "our friendship and aid . . . for Zaire has not been predicated on their perfection in dealing with human rights."[8] In 1979, his assistant secretary of state for Africa, Richard Moose, testified about the dilemmas the United States faced in Zaire; he said:

> On the one hand, there is no way for us to walk away from the problems of Zaire; our interests will not permit it. On the other hand, we cannot restrict our vision to economic self-interest alone. . . . The solution to Zaire's problems obviously depends upon resources from abroad—military, economic, and humanitarian assistance programs. . . . Our policy is to encourage and facilitate reform and recovery by linking our assistance to Zaire's progress in actually implementing changes. We believe our interests in that part of Africa warrant continuation of this policy so long as there is such progress. If there is not, then we should consider policy options other than those we are now pursuing."[9]

But even Moose, the most publicly frank individual to serve as assistant secretary for Africa, was never able to acknowledge that the Mobutu regime was beyond reform. Instead, like a long list of other U.S. officials, he fed the lie that there were real prospects for economic and political progress in Zaire. Washington has persisted in defending the Mobutu regime despite repeated warnings by the United States' most respected experts on Zaire and others who have had direct dealings with Mobutu that it cannot be reformed. (Box 10.1 illustrates the stark differences between administration statements on the prospects for economic and political reform in

Zaire and the assessments of academics and critics of U.S. support for Mobutu.)

Some U.S. officials sincerely believed that quiet diplomatic efforts could have an effect on the Zairian dictator, but many others defended Mobutu knowing full well that they were misleading the American people. The latter group heralded Mobutu's April 24, 1990, announcement that he will permit multiparty elections as a sign that their behind-the-scenes efforts were finally paying off and argued that lifting restrictions on aid to Zaire would permit them to promote democracy more effectively. By September 1991, it was clear that American claims that reforms were underway in Zaire were once again unfounded. If Mobutu is prepared to change his ways and permit democracy and development, it is only because he is no longer confident that those officials and their political allies can win the aid battle in the U.S. Congress and prevent a cutoff of U.S. assistance for his regime.

THE UNITED STATES AND NIMERI

U.S. relations with the Nimeri government in Sudan were more complicated than in the Zaire case. Washington had nothing do with the events that brought Gaafar Nimeri, a former army colonel, to power. When he toppled the Sudan's elected government in May 1969, the American embassy in Khartoum was already closed,* all U.S. aid to the Sudan had been halted, and Washington seemed to be paying little attention to the country.

Initially, Nimeri emulated the radical nationalism of Nasser in Egypt by embracing socialism and turning to Moscow for assistance. But an attempted coup in July 1971 by his erstwhile ally, the Sudan Communist party, caused him to change course and limit his ties to the Soviet Union. In 1971 a tentative rapprochement between the United States and Sudan occurred, but relations between Washington and Khartoum did not improve markedly until Nimeri visited the United States in 1976 to seek

---

* Following the outbreak of the six-day Arab-Israeli war of 1967, the Sudanese government broke diplomatic relations with the United States.

Box 10.1
OFFICIAL U.S. STATEMENTS ON ECONOMIC
AND POLITICAL REFORM IN ZAIRE, 1977 TO 1990

"We believe that our long-range interests in the security and economic via-
bility of Zaire justify the provision of [foreign military sales] credit. Our
proposal comes at a time when *the Government of Zaire is showing every indication
that it is prepared to undertake serious and basic economic reforms** essential to the
economic and financial well-being of the country."

—Richard Moose, Assistant Secretary of State for African Affairs,
March 1978.[1]

" . . . President [Mobutu] has informed me of progress on his government's
economic stabilization plan. *Zaire is taking the difficult but necessary steps to ensure
sustained economic progress,* and it's important that we and Zaire's other friends
do what we can to help."

—President Ronald Reagan, August 1983.[2]

"Zaire is very sensitive to the views of the Administration and the Congress on
human rights, and our concern has had a positive effect. Although Zaire has a
long way to go, *the government has shown it has the capacity to listen to others and
change.*"

—Elliott Abrams, Deputy Assistant Secretary of State for Human Rights,
June 1984.

"We are very enthusiastic about the April 24 speech" [in which Mobutu announced
his intention to carry out political reforms] and especially about the multiparty system. We believe only a multiparty system can lead a developing
country such as Zaire toward true economic growth because this requires the
participation of all of the people. *And if the president's speech is well implemen-
ted . . . then I believe the system can work.*"

—Herman Cohen, Assistant Secretary of State for African Affairs, May
1990.[3]

---

*Emphasis added to all quotes in Box 10.1.
[1]Richard Moose, "Africa: Security Assistance to the Sub-Sahara," *Department of State Bulletin,* Vol. 78, No. 2013, May 1978, p. 30
[2]"Visit of Zaire's President," *Department of State Bulletin,* Vol. 83, No. 2079,
1983, p. 42
[3]Transcript of Press Conference in Kinshasa, May 16, 1990.

STATEMENTS ON ECONOMIC AND POLITICAL CONDITIONS
IN ZAIRE BY ACADEMIC EXPERTS AND POLICY CRITICS

"In reducing the administration's request for FMS credits [to Zaire] by 50 percent, *the subcommittee finds that it is prudent to indicate some gradual disassociation from a corrupt, repressive and clearly unpopular Government* . . . While the subcommittee recognizes that the administration has attempted to use our existing aid program as 'leverage' with the Government of Zaire to bring about meaningful reforms and that constructive changes have taken place during the past year, it also believes that *most reforms to date have been largely cosmetic. . . .*"

Recommendations on U.S. assistance programs of the Africa Subcommittee of the Committee on Foreign Affairs of the House of Representatives, 1980[4]

"[It is] . . . clear that the corruptive system in Zaire with all its wicked and ugly manifestations, its mismanagement and fraud, will destroy all endeavors of international institutions, of friendly governments, and of the commercial banks, towards recovery and rehabilitation of Zaire's economy. Sure, there will be new promises by Mobutu, by members of his government, rescheduling and rescheduling again of a new external public debt, but no (repeat: no) prospect for Zaire's creditors to get their money back in the foreseeable future."

—Erwin Blumenthal, former head of a World Bank team that was sent to Zaire in 1978–79, 1982[5]

"Hope for reform of the present regime is impossible to sustain. Mobutu . . . turns the very weakness of the regime and decay of the state into assets for his own survival. . . . By repressing, dividing, and coopting potential opposition, the regime succeeds in preserving near total uncertainty abroad as to the shape of an alternative political formula, or how it might come into existence. This leaves ample play for the diplomatic community . . . to prefer a hopeless present to an unknowable future. Thus, the Mobutu regime can still extract reluctant, limited, but sufficient backing when mortal peril arises. The crisis—insoluble—continues."

—Professor Crawford Young, 1985[6]

"To believe the Zairian state is now capable of achieving both substantial reform and amelioration in the standard of living of its citizens is a dream. . . ."

—Professor Michael Schatzberg, 1990

---

[4]"Economic and Security Assistance Programs in Africa," Foreign Assistance Legislation for Fiscal Year 1981, Part 7, Subcommittee on Africa, Committee on Foreign Affairs, House of Representatives, 96th Congress, 1980, pp. xiv–xv.
[5]Erwin Blumenthal, "Zaire—Report on Her International Financial Credibility," Typescript, April 7, 1982, cited in Thomas Callaghy, *The State-Society Struggle* (New York: Columbia University Press, 1984), p. 200.
[6]Crawford Young, "The Zairian Crisis and American Foreign Policy," in Gerald Bender et al., *African Crisis Areas and U.S. Foreign Policy* (Berkeley: University of California Press, 1985), p. 223.

American aid and investment. By that time, Nimeri had succeeded in transforming Sudan into an attractive potential ally.

Between 1971 and 1977 (when he could not count on the backing of any external power), Nimeri skillfully defused domestic conflicts and accommodated many of his adversaries. He had inherited a civil war pitting rebels from the predominantly black and Christian southern Sudan against the Muslim- and Arab-dominated government in the north. Fifteen years of fighting (1956–71) had caused roughly half a million Sudanese deaths. Nimeri brought the war to an end by signing the Addis Ababa agreement of February 1972, under which the south became a self-governing region. These accords were and remain unprecedented; no other African leader has made similar concessions. Nimeri also earned considerable praise for reconciling with his political foes in the north. In 1977, he reached an agreement with his principal rival—Sadiq al-Mahdi—that made it possible for opposition forces to participate openly in national politics. Surveying these developments, an American journalist reported in early 1978 that "Nimeri seems to be in better shape domestically than ever before."[10]

In the mid-1970s, Sudan's economic prospects also seemed bright. The economy was growing at a substantially faster rate than that of other African economies. Major economic projects were being launched throughout the country. Arab countries—especially Saudi Arabia and Kuwait—were pouring money into the agricultural sector in hopes of turning Sudan into "the breadbasket of Africa."[11] Reflecting an opinion that was then widely held, a *U.S. News and World Report* article published in September 1977 quoted an American economist as saying "It isn't going to happen overnight, but someday this nation could be the wealthiest country on the continent of Africa."[12]

When Washington began to pay attention to Sudan in the late 1970s, the country thus appeared to be headed in the right direction. But the situation inside Sudan quickly deteriorated. The nation's economy, which had grown at an annual rate of 7 percent between 1973 and 1980, began to decline. Instead of expanding as planned, Sudan's total production of cereals declined by over one-third between 1980 and 1987. And the country's already large external debt doubled between 1980 and 1987, from $5 billion to over $11 billion.

Sudan's economic troubles were paralleled by an equally dramatic political turnaround. Instead of continuing to search for ways to defuse internal conflicts, Nimeri alienated substantial segments of the population by unilaterally abrogating the Addis Ababa accords in June 1983 and imposing Islamic law (Sharia) on the country in September 1983. These actions rekindled the war in the south. Opposition to the Nimeri government increased following the imposition of economic austerity measures required by the IMF as part of a deal to provide continued financial assistance to Sudan. By April 1985, as one expert wrote, "Nimeri had offended nearly all the political and military forces in Sudan."[13] In that month, a series of strikes and protests paralyzed Khartoum, and the Sudanese ruler was ousted by one of his senior military deputies just as he was returning from a visit to the United States.

Was it a coincidence that conditions in Sudan began to deteriorate after the United States started to provide large amounts of assistance to the Nimeri government? How much blame does the United States deserve? It is difficult to provide definitive answers to these questions. The correlation between increasing U.S. aid flows and deteriorating conditions in Sudan is too strong to be dismissed, but the causes are too complex and interwoven for responsibility to be apportioned easily. By any criteria, however, U.S. policy toward Sudan was a failure. It did not accomplish its principal objective—the preservation of a stable pro-Western government in Khartoum. Instead, it contributed to Nimeri's downfall by rewarding him for focusing on external bogeymen such as Libya's Mu'ammar Qadafi and by encouraging him to believe (despite Washington's protests to the contrary) that he could count on U.S. aid to bail him out of his internal political and economic difficulties. A brief review of the evolution of U.S. relations with the Nimeri regime will make it easier to understand these points.

American officials were always more concerned with Khartoum's foreign policy than they were with how well Sudan managed its economy or dealt with its domestic political problems. In

1977–78, the Carter administration decided to sell arms to the Nimeri government and make it the principal African beneficiary of U.S. foreign assistance. This decision was motivated by a perceived need to counter growing Soviet influence in Ethiopia and, more important, a desire to ensure that Khartoum would support U.S.–Egyptian initiatives in the Middle East. In 1980–81, American support for Nimeri was strengthened by his willingness to grant the U.S. military access to his strategically located country in order to facilitate the development of a Persian Gulf rapid deployment force. After the Reagan administration took office, Sudan also became an important base of operations for U.S. efforts to challenge Qadafi. In April 1983, Assistant Secretary of State Crocker summed up U.S. relations with the Nimeri government when he declared that the United States had become "Sudan's closest Western friend."[14]

Between 1979 and 1984, Washington paid almost no attention to deteriorating economic and political conditions in Sudan. Instead, U.S. officials and the Nimeri government echoed each other's arguments that the main threats to Sudan were Ethiopia and Libya. In late 1981, following the assassination of Egyptian leader Anwar Sadat and claims by Nimeri that Qadafi was intensifying efforts to subvert the Khartoum government, the Reagan administration increased military aid to Sudan substantially. "We obviously have a security interest" in Sudan, an administration official told one reporter. "We're going to do whatever we can to make them [the Nimeri government] feel more comfortable, more secure."[15] Most of Nimeri's worst domestic blunders were made after having received such assurances.

By early 1984, the Nimeri regime was facing a serious economic and political crisis. Concerned that U.S. policies were contributing to this crisis, Howard Wolpe, chairman of the Africa subcommittee of the House of Representatives' Committee on Foreign Affairs, conducted a one-day hearing on March 28, 1984. This hearing revealed the underlying flaws in the administration's policy toward Sudan. More generally, it illustrated the problems inherent in the traditional ways in which U.S. policymakers relate to "friendly" but unstable authoritarian regimes in Africa. While acknowledging Sudan's domestic problems, administration officials continued to defend Nimeri. As Box 10.2 shows, their testimony contrasted sharply with that of Douglas Johnson, a leading academic expert on the Sudan.

By late 1984, Sudan's fiscal crisis (brought about by economic mismanagement and heavy defense spending) had become so desperate that the United States froze $200 million of economic aid to Khartoum in hopes of forcing Nimeri to overhaul his country's economy to meet requirements for continued IMF support. "We have no choice," a U.S. official told the *New York Times*. "Even if we wanted to bail him out, we don't have enough money available to do it."[16] But the Reagan administration quickly changed its mind. On April 1, 1985, after a meeting between Nimeri and Reagan in Washington, the White House announced that $67 million would be released because Sudan was taking "the steps required to bring its economy under control." Administration officials also attempted to signal other governments and international agencies that it was "time to be helpful" to the Nimeri government.[17] This action came too late to help the Sudanese leader. Five days after his meeting with President Reagan, Nimeri was ousted.

THE UNITED STATES AND DOE

The United States has a long and blameworthy history of involvement in Liberia dating back to the early nineteenth century. But U.S. policy toward this small West African country was never more pernicious than in the 1980s when American officials spent nearly $500 million to curry favor with—and try to reform—a regime headed by Samuel Doe. As was the case with Mobutu and Nimeri, Washington's investment in Doe yielded nothing but negative long-term returns.

Founded in 1822 by the American Colonization Society, a disparate group of prominent Americans committed to returning freed slaves to Africa, Liberia was the closest thing the United States ever had to a colony on the African continent. In 1847, it became an independent republic. For the next 133 years, an "America-Liberian" oligarchy descended from the roughly

---

Box 10.2
TESTIMONY BY U.S. OFFICIALS ON "SUDAN:
PROBLEMS AND PROSPECTS"[1]

"In examining political stability in the Sudan we must reflect that the country has successfully survived a 17-year civil war and has been beset by many difficulties, not the least of which are severe economic problems and persistent attempts by Libyan leader Qadhafi to overthrow President Nimeri. In consideration of these facts, *the government has done remarkably well.** It has been supportive of our Mideast policy and is pro-west in its orientation. Taking into account the country's turbulent history, it is remarkable that Sudan does not face greater instability." (p. 12)

"Recently . . . relations between north and south [in Sudan] have deteriorated—for a variety of reasons both domestic and international. Against a backdrop of growing economic difficulties, the Sudanese government adopted policies that caused increased disaffection in the south. Restoration of mutual confidence is clearly required. The Nimeri government seeks to deal with the problem politically rather than militarily, and *we are encouraged by the President's March 3 speech, in which he elaborated an accommodating approach to southern demands and renewed efforts to focus on economic development there.*" (p. 7)

"The Government has attempted to protect its garrisons [in the South] but [it] has not attempted to go out after the insurgent bands, adopting rather a policy of political reconciliation. . . . "

Congressman Reid: "It is my understanding that there is also some growing political and military dissidence occurring in the northern part of the country."
Answer: "Nothing of an exceptional nature, Mr. Congressman, it is an enormous country and there are . . . occasional political problems. (pp. 32–33)

". . . There have been some demonstrations at the university, and in all frankness, I am not familiar with the details. Because they were not of such a magnitude as to have been brought very forcibly to Washington's attention." (p. 41)

"*I believe we are on the right track with our policy.* We should continue to counsel political solutions to the problems in the south while working to strengthen the economy and providing the wherewithal for Sudan to be able to protect itself militarily." (p. 18)

---

*Emphasis added to all quotes in Box 10.2.
[1]U.S. Congress. House Subcommittee on Africa, Committee on Foreign Affairs, 98th Congress, Second Session, March 28, 1984.

TESTIMONY BY DOUGLAS JOHNSON ON "SUDAN:
PROBLEMS AND PROSPECTS"

"The U.S. will be making a grave mistake if, for the sake of advancing its own strategic aims in the region, it exaggerates the influence and involvement of its current enemies on the fringes of Sudan's unrest and underestimates the depth of the internal origins of that unrest." (p. 56)

" . . . the Sudan is facing a constitutional crisis which affects the entire country, because it is concerned with the progressive centralization of power in the hands of [President Nimeri], as well as tension between the central and regional governments. In so far as the Southern Sudan is concerned the two problems are related because of the undermining of southern regional autonomy through the intervention of the President." (p. 47)

Congressman Wolpe: "Is there any concrete evidence of . . . initiatives . . . that could restore some momentum toward reconciliation?"
Answer: "As far as I know, there have been no contacts between the Government in Khartoum and the exile movement. And it is only by contacting the leaders of the exile movement that any sort of reconciliation can be guaranteed.

President Nimeri's May 3 address . . . does not recognize . . . that the trust that used to exist between most of the southerners and President Nimeri has been broken by his actions over the last 3 years and it would be very difficult for a new and stronger arrangement to be made between Nimeri and [his] southern . . . opponents because they [can] no longer trust him to keep his word."

. . . I think it is true to say that the Sudanese army is staying in its outposts but it is not because of the deliberate policy of reconciliation. It is because they have been defeated so many times in clashes with the guerrillas that the army itself is rather demoralized." (p. 80)

"President Nimeri's [policies toward the South] must be seen in the context of other actions . . . in Khartoum. He has had increasing contacts with other branches of government and [his own party]. . . . When judges in Khartoum protested last year about the dismissal of a number of their colleagues, he dismissed the judiciary in Khartoum and launched a 'judicial revolution' based on Islamic principles. . . . *The civil service . . . is now reported to be totally inert.*" (pp. 50–51)

"*The hardening of President Nimeri's attitude towards the South has coincided with the increase of U.S. military aid to the Sudan.* . . . There is good reason to believe that this aid has encouraged certain persons in the central government to think that they could depend on U.S. and Egyptian support to suppress any armed opposition that might arise in the Southern Sudan." (pp. 51–52)

20,000 blacks who immigrated to Liberia in the nineteenth century ruled the country.*

Washington has always regarded Liberia as an American preserve. In the early decades of the twentieth century, U.S. officials occasionally intervened to put the country's finances in order and pressure the government in Monrovia to make concessions to U.S. businesses, especially the Firestone Rubber Company. During World War II, the U.S. military used Liberia as a transit point for operations in North Africa and southern Europe. After the war was over, the United States established several critical communications facilities in the country.

From 1944 to 1971, Liberia was governed by President William Tubman. During this period, the country made significant economic gains, but power and wealth remained largely concentrated in the hands of the 5 percent of the population who belonged to the Americo-Liberian group. After Tubman's death, William Tolbert became president. Under Tolbert, corruption, which had always been a serious problem, worsened; the economy deteriorated; and political discontent grew. Despite clear warning signs, U.S. and other officials were caught by surprise when Tolbert was overthrown and brutally murdered in April 1980 by a handful of noncommissioned officers led by Master-Sergeant Samuel Doe.

Washington reacted to the coup with a combination of alarm and discomfiture. Administration officials worried that the new regime might turn to the Soviet Union or Libya for assistance. Some of them were also genuinely troubled by Liberia's past. Testifying before Congress in August 1980, Assistant Secretary of State for African Affairs Moose was somewhat sympathetic with Doe and the others responsible for the coup. He explained that they came from neglected rural areas and shared "a strong sense of grievance toward the Americo-Liberian elite" based on their resentment "of the corruption in the Tolbert government and of the general indifference of the ruling elite to the plight of the people at large."[18] These concerns (and an overstated fear

---

* Although called Americo-Liberians, not all of these immigrants came from the United States. They were a mix of former slaves and free-born blacks from the United States and others who were released before reaching the United States.

that U.S. "credibility in the eyes of Europeans and Africans" was at stake) caused the Carter administration to rush a package of economic and military aid for the new regime through the congressional appropriations process. "If we act promptly," Moose told Congress, "we will be in a position to be of assistance at a relatively modest cost and to exercise influence on the course of events." But, he warned, "There is no assurance our proposed strategy will succeed."[19]

The Reagan administration significantly increased U.S. support for the Doe government in a number of ways. One of the first things it did was send one hundred soldiers from the U.S. Army Special Forces to Liberia to train Doe's troops. "You're dealing with a sergeant," a State Department official told reporters. "He'll take us more seriously if there's a military dimension to our aid."[20] Reports that Libya was courting the new Liberian regime spurred this move. Doe quickly allayed Washington's fears by closing the Libyan embassy in Monrovia, forcing Moscow to reduce the size of its embassy staff, and purging his regime of individuals who were perceived as radicals. In August 1981, Doe accused five "left-leaning" members of the regime's seventeen-man ruling People's Redemption Council, including its co-chairman, Thomas Weh-Schn, of plotting a coup and executed them. Weh-Sehn had been a leading critic of the decisions to close the Libyan mission and develop close ties with the United States.[21]

The August executions alarmed many Liberians. One journalist reported that "a climate of fear has taken hold in this West African capital following the most recent executions of purported coup plotters and the accumulation of unchallenged power by . . . Doe."[22] U.S. officials viewed things differently. In a speech to the Liberian Shipowners Association in Houston, Texas, two months after the executions, William Swing, the American ambassador in Monrovia, noted that the Doe government was "genuinely concerned about possible countercoups" and declared that "we want to assure the government of our support for its basic security."[23] The Reagan administration hoped that such reassurances would enhance their ability to reform the Doe government.

Between 1981 and 1985, U.S. officials diligently tutored the poorly educated master-sergeant on international politics and constitutional reform. Throughout this period, Assistant Secretary Crocker argued that Liberia was firmly on the road to democracy. In April 1983, for example, he boldly declared that "Liberia represents the best prospect in Africa, and one of the best in the world, for rapid movement toward democracy."[24] Crocker maintained this position long after most experts on Liberia had concluded that Doe could not be reformed.[25]

A watershed was reached in October 1985 when long-awaited national elections were held. After early returns indicated that he was losing, Doe stopped the vote count and set up a special election commission loaded with his allies. Two weeks later, it declared Doe the victor by a suspiciously narrow majority of 50.9 percent. These results were roundly denounced. Only Crocker could find anything positive to say about the election. In testimony before the Senate Foreign Relations Committee, he refused to admit that Doe had stolen the election. Instead, the assistant secretary made a laughable argument that "the prospects for national reconciliation were brightened by Doe's claim that he won only a narrow 51 percent election victory. . . . "[26] The October election charade doomed the Reagan administration's policy. As happened in the case of South Africa, Crocker's arguments for what many analysts perceived as "constructive engagement" with the Doe government lost their credibility. The evidence now weighed too heavily in favor of those who argued that Doe had no intention of giving up power. But the administration refused to change course until it was forced to do so by Congress. (Box 10.3 compares the arguments used by administration officials to defend U.S. aid to the Doe regime with critical assessments of American policy.)

Secretary of State George Shultz astounded most Liberians during a January 1987 visit to Monrovia by saying that he thought the country was making "genuine progress" toward greater democracy.[27] Less than a month later, the U.S. General Accounting Office released an audit claiming that millions of dollars of U.S. aid to Liberia had been diverted and misused by officials in the Doe government. Under growing bipartisan pressure from the U.S. Congress, the administration attempted to salvage its policy by sending an AID team to take over management of Liberia's finances.[28] In late 1988, after it became clear that they could not control Doe's personal financial excesses, the team left,[29] leaving the administration with no choice but to cut U.S. aid to Liberia.

In December 1989, rebels from the Ivory Coast led by a former Liberian military officer, Charles Taylor, started a guerrilla war against the Doe regime. By then, however, senior officials in Washington had forgotten their earlier reasons for being interested in Liberia. As the war escalated, State Department spokesman Richard Boucher declared that "the administration believes that it's not our role to intervene, to engage in peacekeeping or to impose a government or political system in Liberia."[30] In late 1990, U.S. marines were deployed off the coast of Liberia, but only to evacuate American citizens and safeguard U.S. property.

When pressed to defend past U.S. policy, Assistant Secretary Cohen argued in 1990 that the United States was blameless. Despite Washington's best efforts, "Doe was just not able to come around to do the correct thing."[31] In similar fashion, after Doe was overthrown and murdered, Cohen criticized the insurgents for not taking advantage of concessions that the United States had extracted from the Liberian dictator.[32] What is totally missing from the official record is any acknowledgment that U.S. policy contributed to the tragedy that has befallen Liberia by providing aid, counsel, and legitimacy to Master-Sergeant Doe. As in the cases of Sudan and Zaire, U.S. policy toward Liberia failed—and Africans paid the price.

PROSPECTS FOR THE FUTURE

With the end of the Cold War, many people expect the United States to abandon the policies that produced past failures such as those in Liberia, Sudan, and Zaire. This could happen, but there is no guarantee that it will. Containing communism was only one of several rationales used to justify American involvement in

---

BOX 10.3
OFFICIAL U.S. STATEMENTS ON LIBERIA, 1985–1991

"We have been active over the past five years in encouraging Liberian authorities to usher in a new day in Liberia*. . . . These efforts were centered on holding elections in October of 1985 for a return to civilian rule in January of 1986. There were a number of criticisms of the October elections, and we share some of them, as the Liberian Government knows, but the elections had some positive aspects as well. Four political parties competed in an open election campaign that was covered by a variety of newspapers, not all of them government owned. . . . Large numbers of Liberians went to the polls on election day, which by all accounts were free and open. As you know, the vote itself was counted behind closed doors by a government-appointed commission of some 50 people drawn from various walks of life. This performance established a beginning, however imperfect, that Liberia and its friends would use as a benchmark for the future, one on which they want to build."

—Chester Crocker, Assistant Secretary of State for African Affairs, December 1985[1]

"We believe there is reason to keep trying to work with the Doe government to make the promise of Liberia's Second Republic succeed. There is in Liberia today a civilian government, a multiparty legislature, a journalistic community of government and nongovernment newspapers and radio stations, and an ongoing tradition among the citizenry of speaking out, a new constitution that protects freedoms and a judicial system that can help enforce those provisions. The Government is committed publicly to that system."

—Chester Crocker, Assistant Secretary of State for African Affairs, January 1986[2]

"In Liberia there has been some improvement in political conditions, and the 1986 municipal elections were apparently conducted in a fair and open manner. But much mistrust still lingers over the 1985 national elections and subsequent coup attempt, and *the Liberian Government is working to overcome the effects of earlier press bannings and repression against opposition groups. We have welcomed these developments and are urging further progress in dealing with the problems that remain."*

—Roy Stacy, Deputy Assistant Secretary of State for African Affairs, March 1987[3]

---

*Emphasis added to all quotes in Box 10.3.
[1] Testimony, "Liberia and United States Policy," hearings, Subcommittee on Africa, Committee on Foreign Affairs, House of Representatives, Ninety-Ninth Congress, December 10, 1985, pp. 1–2.
[2] Testimony, "Liberia: Recent Developments and United States Foreign Policy," hearings, Subcommittees on Human Rights and International Organization and on Africa, Committee on Foreign Affairs, House of Representatives, Ninety-Ninth Congress, January 23, 1986, p. 38.
[3] Roy Stacy, "FY 1988 Assistance Requests for Sub-Sahara Africa," *Department of State Bulletin,* Vol. 87, No. 2122, May 1987, p. 16.

CRITICAL VIEWS OF U.S. POLICY TOWARD LIBERIA

"After the April 12, 1980, coup, the . . . United States initiated a policy to help stabilize Liberia and bring about civilian rule. The administration proposed to . . . help stabilize the economy, provide for a well trained and disciplined army and prepare the country for return to civilian rule through free, open multiparty elections. . . . It hoped to influence Dr. Doe's government through quiet diplomacy. *This policy of constructive engagement in Liberia has not worked.* Economically, Liberia is in such serious financial difficulties that it borders on collapse. . . . The army is now . . . a group of well-trained men who have almost absolute power to intimidate, arrest, beat and even execute Liberian citizens. Before the United States entered the scene with its massive aid, Liberians were concerned with issues such as freedom of speech. Now they fear for their very lives."

—Reverend Thomas Hayden, January 1986[4]

The United States continued through the time of difficulties in 1985–86 to provide the formalities that are so dear to the heart of the Liberians—such as warm words of praise and assurances of continued economic support when the new U.S. ambassador presented his credentials; Reagan's congratulatory messages to Doe after the October election and following the failure of [a November 1985] coup attempt; and the dispatching of an official delegation (albeit at a lower level) to the inauguration of Doe. On the other hand, the Department of State, and even the Congress, avoided doing those things which would have signaled deep concern and displeasure. . . . *When Chester Crocker or a State Department spokesman did comment on developments, it was often in a way that undermined the effectiveness of the opposition to Doe."*

—J. Gus Liebenow, 1987[5]

"There exists in Liberia today the widespread perception that the Reagan Administration bent over backwards to rationalize rights abuses and to overlook clear evidence of widespread electoral fraud in 1985 The Administration's policy engendered a sense of betrayal among Liberians across a broad spectrum. Many believed that the United States, having failed in its earlier efforts to support democratic change in their country, cast its lot with President Doe, ignoring flagrant abuses by his armed forces and government."

—Michael Posner, June 1990[6]

---

[4]"Liberia: Recent Developments and United States Foreign Policy," Subcommittee on Human Rights and International Organizations, Committee on Foreign Affairs, House of Representatives, 99th Congress, January 23, 1986, p. 38.

[5]*Liberia: The Quest for Democracy* (Bloomington: Indiana University Press, 1987), pp. 34–35.

[6]"U.S. Policy and the Crisis in Liberia," hearing, Subcommittee on Africa, Committee on Foreign Affairs, House of Representatives, 101st Congress, U.S. Government Printing Office, Washington D.C., 1990.

those three countries—and not always the most important one in the minds of the officials most responsible for formulating and implementing U.S. policy. While the need to counter Moscow can no longer be used to justify the foreign policy bureaucracy's preference for quiet diplomacy and constructive engagement, other rationales can and almost certainly will be employed to defend the use of these traditional diplomatic practices in dealings with future Does, Mobutus, and Nimeris. The Pentagon's emphasis on the threat posed by instability in the Third World is particularly worrisome in this regard. But even if geopolitical factors do not regain currency, there are a multitude of more country-specific rationales that can be used to rationalize old approaches. This is already happening.

Although Assistant Secretary Cohen has emphasized the post–Cold War commitment of the United States to democracy in Africa, the Bush administration has resisted congressional pressure to reduce aid to African dictators. In April 1989, for example, Deputy Assistant Secretary of State Alison Rosenberg argued against cuts in assistance to Kenya, Somalia, and Zaire with a warning that "should we be unable to sustain necessary assistance levels, we risk the collapse or delay of economic reforms, injury to friendly governments, and acrimonious charges of a breach of faith."[33] Somalia provides a particularly egregious example of the bureaucracy's ability to generate rationales for continued U.S. ties with corrupt and repressive regimes.

Throughout the 1980s, U.S. aid to Mogadishu was clearly understood as a quid pro quo arrangement. Somalia got aid, in return for which the U.S. military got access and facilities. By 1989, most analysts had concluded both that Somalia was no longer strategically important and that the Barre regime was doomed. Nevertheless, officials in the Bush administration continued to argue that the United States should assist the Somali government. The rationales given for continued aid varied, depending on the audience and agency being represented. In February 1989, for example, Deputy Assistant Secretary of State Kenneth Brown testified before the House Foreign Affairs Committee, "We believe it is very important that the United States remain engaged in Somalia in order to keep . . . momentum [on human rights] going. We need to show our support for positive change while continuing to press for further improvements."[34] One year later, a then little-known general, H. Norman Schwarzkopf, who headed the U.S. Central Command, argued before the House Appropriations Committee that "maintaining a United States military presence in Somalia and continuing our military relationship, even if security assistance is confined to non-lethal items, allows us to maintain valuable contacts, counterbalances the growing relationship between Somalia and Libya, and helps Somalia maintain its political and territorial integrity."[35] Fortunately, most members of Congress were not persuaded by either of these arguments, and they prevented the Bush administration from being tempted to organize a last-minute rescue operation to forestall the collapse of the Barre regime.*

Developments in Kenya in 1990–91 provide another depressing bit of evidence that the predispositions of U.S. officials have not changed. This is the one African country that has presented the Bush administration with a clear opportunity to abandon traditional diplomatic practices—but the administration has refused to do so. In the past two years, as Africa Watch and other monitoring groups have documented, human rights violations in Kenya have increased. The Bush administration has condemned some of the abuses, especially the jailing of prominent journalists and human rights lawyers. But much as the Reagan administration did in the case of South Africa, it has done so in isolated and circumscribed ways, and only under pressure from Congress. The one major exception occurred in early 1990, when the U.S. ambassador to Kenya—a crusty and distinctly undiplomatic conservative ex-journalist, Smith Hempstone—touched off a political firestorm in Nairobi by mildly

---

* A final footnote on this sad saga was provided by a January 1991 letter to the *Washington Post* by T. Frank Crigler, who served as U.S. ambassador to Somalia during the worst years of Barre's tenure. Denying that the United States had played a major role in arming the Barre regime, Crigler argued, "We not only disappointed Siad . . . but we also emboldened his critics by condemning the regime's human rights violations and by urging democratic reforms." With Barre on the run, thousands of Somalis dead, and the country in total chaos, Crigler's prescription was to reopen the U.S. embassy. ("Once the smoke clears, Somalis are going to need help. Our diplomats should be back in place on that embassy compound, ready to lend a hand.")

endorsing the Kenyan opposition's call for the establishment of a multiparty democracy. President Moi and his supporters denounced Hempstone, and Kenyan activists briefly entertained hopes that Washington would distance itself from the Moi government. But their hopes were soon dashed.

In August 1990, Assistant Secretary Cohen visited Nairobi. During his brief stay, Cohen refused to meet with human rights monitors or the relatives of political detainees, and he declined to criticize the Moi regime publicly. As Africa Watch later reported, "Cohen's visit strengthened President Moi's hand at a time of mounting pressure for Kenya to democratize, sending a clear message that the United States was not going to press human rights concerns. This stance only helped to facilitate the serious deterioration of respect for human rights that followed."[36]

In February 1991, the Bush administration released $5 million of aid to Kenya that had been suspended by the U.S. Congress. The stated reason for this action was the Moi government's support for U.S. policy during the Persian Gulf war and improvements in its human rights record. But it was later revealed that an additional objective was to convince President Moi to provide a home for 350 Libyan exiles who had fled Chad where they were being trained by the CIA to launch a guerrilla war against Qadafi. (Washington turned to Moi after Mobutu booted the Libyans out of Zaire when Congress rejected an administration plan to give his regime the $5 million for taking the homeless would-be insurgents.)[37]

11

MODELS OF SUCCESS

In the fall of 1984, while the U.S. foreign policy Establishment was busy debating the significance of signals emanating from Moscow, events in Ethiopia and South Africa catapulted the continent to the top of the American foreign policy agenda. In early September, protests against a new South African constitution entrenching white rule sparked violent confrontations in black townships. Scenes of white policemen beating black protesters became standard fare on American television news programs. Then, in late October, the NBC *Nightly News* broadcast pictures of starving women and children dying by the hundreds in Ethiopia. The American public responded to the Ethiopian famine immediately, contributing millions of dollars to relief agencies virtually overnight. It reacted to the drama in South Africa a little more slowly, but with no less force. By the end of the year, thousands of Americans were demonstrating against apartheid outside of South African embassies and consulates across the country and condemning the Reagan administration's policy of "constructive engagement." The sudden upsurge of public concern about suffering in these two distant countries overwhelmed official Washington.

In October 1984, images of dying Ethiopian children spawned a broad domestic constituency favoring emergency relief programs. Private voluntary organizations such as Catholic Relief Services (CRS), Save the Children, and World Vision greatly expanded their operations in Ethiopia. Members of Congress took a personal interest in monitoring relief operations and ensuring an adequate flow of food and other needed supplies. And the Reagan administration was forced to put aside its concerns that relief assistance might bolster the Marxist regime headed by President Mengistu Haile Mariam and undertake a massive effort to feed starving Ethiopians.

After being largely ignored by senior officials for nearly two years, the Ethiopian famine rocketed to the top of the Reagan administration's foreign policy agenda in a matter of weeks. Washington was first warned about a possible famine in late 1982. By early 1984, private relief agencies (especially CRS), officials in the U.S. Agency for International Development (USAID), and the American embassy staff in Addis Ababa were all pushing for increased relief assistance to the country.[1] Their lobbying produced significant but incremental increases in the flow of U.S. emergency aid. But Washington failed to attach any urgency to the situation until after the October 1984 NBC News broadcast.

During congressional hearings held in mid-September 1984, M. Peter McPherson, administrator of USAID, did not mention the possibility that millions of lives were potentially at risk in Ethiopia. In prepared testimony on emergency food assistance to Africa, he merely noted that "the failure of the rains to start on time (later compensated by heavy rains) will not help that country improve its already perilous condition." When pressed to defend the relatively small amount of U.S. assistance being provided to Ethiopia, McPherson admitted that "it wasn't altogether popular in this Government to get food to Ethiopia. . . . " But he insisted that the administration was providing "as much food there as we could get delivered in some credible way." The problem, he argued, was basically the result of the policies being followed by the Soviet-backed regime in Addis Ababa.[2]

But once the American public began expressing an interest in the fate of the Ethiopians, the Reagan administration quickly adopted a visible public posture on famine relief. On October 30, the White House issued a statement on food assistance to Ethiopia. "As you know," it began, "the President has taken a personal interest in the famine situation in Africa, particularly the current crisis in Ethiopia."[3] In contrast with McPherson's testimony six weeks earlier, the White House statement discussed U.S. aid to Ethiopia extensively, announcing that $45 million had been committed to the relief effort. By the end of the year, Washington had increased the total amount of funds committed to the Ethiopian relief effort to more than $125 million. Then, on January 3,

1985, the president announced "a comprehensive African hunger relief initiative" that would provide more than $1 billion in food aid and disaster relief to the continent as a whole.[4] Testifying before Congress on January 17, 1985, Assistant Secretary of State for Africa Chester Crocker argued that "the United States has mounted an unprecedented campaign to provide assistance to Africa in its current hour of need." Significantly, he felt it necessary to deny that relief policies were influenced by Cold War considerations, claiming, "We have not allowed political or ideological differences with any government to weaken our determination to have assistance reach those in need."[5] While the change that occurred in U.S. policy regarding Ethiopia was substantial, it was generally consistent with the administration's already existing famine relief policy. The White House had announced a modest program to combat world hunger in July 1984. Public pressure affected policy by silencing hard-line critics of the Ethiopian relief effort and causing the administration to provide large amounts of emergency aid to an ideologically hostile country. But a far more radical shift occurred vis-à-vis South Africa. There public pressure forced the Reagan administration to abandon totally its strategy of constructive engagement.*

When Assistant Secretary Crocker first officially outlined the rationale for constructive engagement in August 1981, he did so in explicitly geopolitical terms. Southern Africa, he argued, "is an increasingly contested arena in global politics. . . . It is imperative that we play our proper role in fostering the region's security and countering the expansion of Soviet influence." While insisting that the administration would not align itself with "apartheid policies," Crocker sent a carefully phrased message clearly directed at the African National Congress (ANC) and other black liberation movements fighting against Pretoria. "We will not," he warned, "lend our voice to support those dedicated to seizing and holding power through violence." Instead, Crocker explained, "we need policies that sustain those who would resist the siren call of violence and the blandishments

---

* Constructive engagement, as conceived by Assistant Secretary Crocker, was nothing more than an elaborate and more systematic form of the traditional diplomatic practices that were examined in Chapter 10.

of Moscow and its clients."[6] In a key passage, he spelled out the logic underlying administration thinking:

> We cannot and will not permit our hand to be forced to align ourselves with one side or the other in [southern Africa's] disputes. Our task . . . is to maintain communication with all parties . . . and to pursue our growing interests throughout the region. Only if we engage constructively in southern Africa as a whole can we play our proper role in the search for negotiated solutions, peaceful change, and expanding economic progress. In South Africa, the region's dominant country, it is not our task to choose between black and white. . . . We recognize that a measure of change is already underway in South Africa. At such a time, when many South Africans of all races, in and out of government, are seeking to move away from apartheid, it is our task to be supportive of this process so that proponents of reform and nonviolent change can gain and hold the initiative.[7]

Crocker's superiors spoke in less guarded or nuanced terms. Testifying before Congress during his confirmation hearing in January 1981, Secretary of State–designate Alexander Haig commented that "it is in our interest, of course, to bring about a solution [in South Africa] which is not going to put in jeopardy the interest of those who share our values and . . . strategic sense."[8] Six weeks later, President Reagan put it more bluntly in a closely watched television interview when he asked, "Can we abandon a country that has stood beside us in every war we've ever fought, a country that strategically is essential to the free world . . . ? I just feel that . . . if we're going to sit down at a table with the Russians, surely we can keep the door open and continue to negotiate with a friendly nation like South Africa."[9]

Despite steady criticism from liberals in Congress and a determined grass-roots campaign by antiapartheid activists, the Reagan administration maintained the ability to guide U.S. relations with South Africa for most of its first term in office. Then, in late 1984, several cracks appeared in the dike that was holding back opposition to constructive engagement. In early September, a barrage of news stories about black protests and white brutality undercut the administration's claims that positive reforms were underway in the land of apartheid. In October, Bishop Desmond Tutu, an articulate and personable church leader, was awarded the Nobel Peace prize for his efforts to end apartheid. He promptly used his new platform to accuse the Reagan administration of doing "precious little to advance" the struggle against white rule. "If anything," he charged, "it has assisted in making the South African government more intransigent."[10]

On November 22, 1984, while most Americans prepared to sit down to a traditional Thanksgiving dinner, three black political leaders, including Congressman Walter Fauntroy of the District of Columbia, seized the opportunity created by the extensive news coverage of the unrest in South Africa and Tutu's well publicized charges to begin a sit-in at the South African embassy in Washington, D.C., protesting apartheid and constructive engagement. Following their arrest, a flood tide of public protest rolled across the country. By mid-1985, thousands of protesters, including many prominent political leaders, trade unionists, athletes, and television stars had been arrested outside the South African embassy. Demonstrations calling for an end to U.S. investment in South Africa took place on most major college campuses. Hundreds of state and local governments, public pension funds, and universities adopted their own sanctions against companies doing business with South Africa. Members of Congress, including moderate Republicans such as Senators Nancy Kassebaum and Richard Lugar and conservatives such as Representatives Newt Gingrich and Jack Kemp, rushed to associate themselves with antiapartheid legislation.

For two years, the Reagan administration fought desperately to prevent Congress from limiting its options regarding South Africa. It attempted to co-opt Congress in September 1985 by enacting economic sanctions that it had previously opposed through an executive order. It created a special State Department working group to mount a public relations campaign. It also appointed a high-level advisory committee to the secretary of state that it mistakenly hoped would recommend against sanctions. It stopped using the phrase "constructive engagement." And it nominated a black American to be ambassador to South Africa. But none of these maneuvers worked. In October 1986, Congress overrode a presidential veto by a resounding margin to pass a far-reaching sanctions bill: the Comprehensive Anti-Apartheid Act.[11]

Throughout the debate over South Africa, the sanctions issue received most of the public attention. Yet the most telling shift in U.S. policy involved the administration's relations with the ANC, the oldest and most popular antiapartheid movement in South Africa. Prior to 1986, official American contacts with black opposition movements were deliberately limited, largely because of the perception that the ANC and its close ally, the South African Communist Party (SACP), were aligned with Moscow. In a nationally televised speech in July 1986, President Reagan followed the advice of hard-liners in the White House and tried to undermine the antiapartheid movement by directly attacking the ANC. While expressing his belief in the need for an end to apartheid, the president harshly criticized the ANC. After referring to "the calculated terror by elements of the African National Congress," he said that "the South African government has a right and responsibility to maintain order in the face of terrorists." Later in the speech, he declared that Pretoria "is under no obligation to negotiate the future of the country with any organization that proclaims a goal of creating a Communist state and uses terrorist tactics and violence to achieve it." Calling South Africa "one of the most [strategically] vital regions of the world," the president warned, "The Soviet Union is not unaware of the stakes."[12] At the height of the Cold War, warnings such as these would have been sufficient to scare many members of Congress away from voting against the president's policy. But as U.S. relations with Moscow continued to improve, it became ever more difficult for the Reagan administration to use the Communist threat in an attempt to disarm its critics. By 1985–86, most senators and congressmen were at least as worried about being labeled "soft on racism" as they were about being declared "soft on communism."

Testifying before Congress the day after the president's July 1986 speech, Secretary of State George Shultz bowed to changing political realities and announced that he would meet with senior ANC officials. In January 1987, he met with ANC president Oliver Tambo in Washington, ushering in a new era in U.S. relations with the black opposition in South Africa. Three years later, millions of Americans welcomed the release from prison of the ANC's most celebrated hero, Nelson Mandela, even though Mandela steadfastly refused to distance himself from the SACP.

In addition to forcing changes in official policy, many Americans chose to take private action to assist Ethiopian famine victims and to help the victims of apartheid in South Africa. Acting through the myriad of private agencies and associations discussed in Chapter 9, they sent money, volunteered their services, and set up exchange programs.

In Ethiopia, long before the U.S. government began to respond to the 1984 crisis, nearly forty private voluntary organizations were running a wide range of programs. They played a critical role in getting news of the famine to the American public. Their workers, many of them Ethiopians hired locally, helped to document the severity of the famine; and their logistical support enabled journalists to report the story. In addition, they lobbied Congress and the executive branch for more relief aid. When aid began to flow into the country, private agencies such as CRS, CARE, Lutheran World Services, and World Vision and their local counterparts assumed responsibility for transporting and distributing relief supplies. Without the private voluntary organizations (PVOs) and the local infrastructure they helped to build, Washington would not have been able to respond effectively to the famine crisis. Just as important, while the U.S. government strictly limited its operations to the provision of emergency relief, private groups set up programs to address longer-term needs. Because of the efforts of the PVOs, thousands of Ethiopians were employed and trained, thus greatly enhancing the country's human infrastructure. Moreover, the international relief effort did not help President Mengistu to survive, as some U.S. officials had feared that it would. Instead, it helped to reduce the dependence of the Ethiopian people on Addis Ababa. By focusing attention on the failures of the regime to provide for its citizens, the relief effort also helped to discredit Mengistu's policies and to embarrass his supporters. In these ways, the PVOs indirectly contributed to the May 1991 collapse of his government.

A handful of private American groups had been working to promote change in South Africa since the early 1960s. In the mid-1980s, they were joined by a host of others. While Congress debated whether or not to impose economic sanctions and the Reagan administration sought to maintain communication with Pretoria, universities, private associations, and trade unions sought ways to assist the black majority directly. The University of California system created an internship program for black community activists. Other American colleges and universities created scholarship programs and lectureships. Legal organizations, such as the Lawyer's Committee for Civil Rights under Law, raised money to support legal aid clinics and to defend political prisoners. The UAW (United Automobile, Aerospace and Agricultural Implement Workers of America), the UMW (United Mineworkers of America), AFSCME (American Federation of State, County and Municipal Employees), and other American unions established programs to help independent black trade unions in South Africa. Churches across the United States raised money to support community programs run by their South African counterparts. In the process, literally thousands of personal links were created between Americans and South Africans, links that will survive the end of apartheid.

During the mid-1980s debate over South Africa, many executive branch officials and foreign policy experts publicly lamented the seeming confusion and incoherence caused by the challenges to their control over U.S. policy. In April 1985, as public opposition to constructive engagement was spreading, secretary of State George Shultz called for "a national consensus" on southern Africa. "We simply cannot afford to let southern Africa become a divisive domestic issue," he argued. "As long as Americans speak with contrary and confusing voices," the secretary declared, "our influence will be less than it could be."[13] Four years later, the Bush administration's leading Africanist, Assistant Secretary of State Herman Cohen, retrospectively endorsed Shultz's judgment. Testifying before Congress on the effectiveness of the Comprehensive Anti-Apartheid Act in October 1989, he called South Africa "an area where the breakdown of bipartisan support undercut the ability of the United States to encourage a peaceful transition to democracy."[14] By early 1990, it was clear that this official judgment was being proven wrong.

The domestic American debate over South Africa—and the policy that it brought about—played an important role in helping to create the conditions that led President F. W. de Klerk to release ANC leader Mandela and to begin negotiations that will inevitably lead to the demise of white rule. Eventually, internal political and economic forces would no doubt have caused the collapse of apartheid. But so many white South Africans would not have come to their senses as quickly as they did had the American people not forced the Reagan administration to abandon its policy of constructive engagement. Moreover, the various programs that have been established recently by private American groups to assist black South Africans have strengthened civil society in that country in ways that will greatly improve the prospects for the eventual emergence of a stable, multiracial democracy.

It is doubtful that any African problem will soon receive the amount of attention or generate as much U.S. public concern as the Ethiopian famine and apartheid issues did in the mid-1980s. But that does not mean that the successes achieved in these two cases cannot be used as models for future American policies.

12

STRENGTHENING CIVIL SOCIETY
IN AFRICA

Before there can be any hope of changing U.S. policy toward Africa, Americans must conduct a plain-spoken and self-critical debate that considers all of the newly available strategic options. One strategy would be simply to ignore Africa in a deliberate and systematic manner. A second possibility would be to attempt to "save" Africa with American ideas and resources. Yet neither one of these strategies could be sustained for long.

In the post–Cold War era, the natural impulse of the foreign policy Establishment is to ignore Africa. Given that U.S. strategic and economic interests in Africa are not significant and that in those places where the United States has been most involved it has usually done more harm than good, it might be in the best interests of both Americans and Africans if the United States was to pursue a policy of benign neglect toward the continent. But that will not happen.

The foreign policy Establishment remains firmly committed to the idea that the United States is a global power with responsibilities reaching out to all parts of the world. This belief makes it difficult for even those senior officials who have no interest in Africa to advocate a deliberate policy of benign neglect. Moreover, even if they were willing to embrace such an approach, their Africanist deputies and domestic constituencies would keep the United States involved in the continent's affairs.

When senior American officials ignore Africa, U.S. policy initiatives (and African interests) are left to the mercy of whichever bureaucrat or constituency group happens to gain control over a particular issue. Whether a country receives aid, whether a humanitarian crisis attracts Washington's attention, whether an African dictator continues to receive American backing, all come to depend on ephemeral and often arbitrary factors. A famine in Ethiopia that makes it into the media spotlight becomes an international *cause célèbre* while equally devastating famines in other African countries go unnoticed. Nations and political organizations with effective lobbyists and powerful friends remain in good favor with Washington, while those that are too poor and unimportant to afford lobbyists or attract powerful friends are ignored. Human rights issues or environmental causes that are taken up by influential American groups get on the U.S. policy agenda; others do not.

Ignoring Africa thus becomes a recipe for haphazard involvement. U.S. interests are not served; and Africa is not helped. Instead, more often than not, American resources are squandered.

It also would be a mistake to pretend that the United States can lead a crusade to save Africa from poverty, political repression, and civil war. Attempting to do so would require a stock of ideas, resources, and, most of all, a degree of commitment that Washington does not possess.

The belief that American ideas about democracy, economics, and world order can be retailed cheaply abroad is dangerous. Transforming undemocratic political systems, reforming collapsed economies, and ending civil wars are extremely difficult tasks, especially in Africa. If Washington were to take on these challenges, it would have to commit extraordinarily large amounts of money and manpower. The only precedents for such an effort are the postwar reconstruction of Europe and Japan.

Yet "saving" Africa would be far more expensive and difficult than the postwar reconstruction efforts. For example, many economists estimate that South Africa alone will need an immediate infusion of $10 billion in foreign capital to establish an economic base that will allow a postapartheid democracy to survive and prosper. The costs of reconstructing war-devastated Angola, Ethiopia, Liberia, Mozambique, and Somalia would be even greater, and with far less prospect of short-term payoffs. Given the backlog of U.S. domestic needs—and the clear evidence that the American people are not eager to see U.S. taxpayer dollars spent abroad—it is unrealistic to expect Washington to commit the resources that will be needed in these areas.

Without the financial resources to back them up, efforts by U.S. officials to promote democracy and to encourage the spread of free-market capitalism are not likely to succeed. Worse, such efforts may get in the way of African attempts to take responsibility for coming up with their own solutions. As long as the illusion exists that the United States will take on Africa's burdens, African leaders will have an incentive to delay making the sacrifices that will be necessary if the continent is to right itself.

If the United States can neither ignore Africa nor save it, what should Americans do? The best strategy would be to find ways to encourage Africans to develop their own ideas and to mobilize their own resources to deal with the continent's problems. Instead of launching additional high-profile initiatives such as the Economic Policy Initiative of 1984–85 or the Democracy Initiative of 1990–91, U.S. officials and other Americans concerned about the continent should undertake to strengthen the various groups that comprise African civil society, in the same ways that Americans have helped to strengthen civil society in Ethiopia and South Africa.

STRENGTHENING AFRICAN CIVIL SOCIETY

Africa's ongoing crises have many dimensions, but most of them derive from the imbalance that exists between the state and civil society. Since independence, African rulers have operated free from the checks provided by a strong civil society. This problem has been noted by a broad and diverse group of observers. For example, in a widely read 1989 report, the World Bank noted: "Because countervailing power has been lacking, state officials in many countries have served their own interests without fear of being called to account."[1]

International power politics has fostered the imbalance between the state and civil society in Africa. More than anywhere else in the world, states in Africa are products of the international system. Their boundaries are largely the result of bargains struck among imperialist rivals at the Congress of Berlin in 1884–85. The rights and prerogatives they enjoy derive from norms the great powers established at the Paris Peace Conference in 1919 and the San Francisco Conference in 1945. Since their independence, African states have been nourished by international agencies and financial institutions and protected by one or another of the great powers. "The survival of Africa's existing states," as political scientists Robert Jackson and Carl Rosberg have argued, "is largely an international achievement."[2]

Until recently, Africa's rulers could count on support from a diverse mix of sources. Many Africanists endorsed the argument that one-party states represented a uniquely African form of democracy, thus legitimizing the rulers' efforts to suppress political opposition. Many American conservatives portrayed authoritarian rule as a natural and (as long as the dictators did not embrace communism) unobjectionable product of Africa's backwardness. By emphasizing government-to-government relations and sustaining the pretensions of African rulers, traditional diplomatic practices reinforced the imbalance that exists between state and society in Africa. Also foreign assistance mostly served, as the conservative British economist P. T. Bauer has argued, to "increase the resources and power of recipient governments compared with the rest of society."[3]

Thus, the main effect of international involvement in Africa in the postindependence era has been to assist African rulers to consolidate their power and insulate themselves from the demands and pressures of civil society. As long as those who control the African state apparatus are assured of the support of the international community, they have little reason to worry about the civil rights, health, or prosperity of their own people. It is unfortunately possible for most people living in a country to suffer tremendously without the power and privileges of the ruling elites being affected at all.

To help correct these imbalances, the United States can do two things. First, it can adopt guidelines to ensure that Washington will no longer provide aid and comfort to African dictators or otherwise favor the state at the expense of civil society. On a more positive note, it could take steps that would strengthen the desire and capacity of the associations and groups that comprise American civil society—Drucker's "third sector"—to assist their African counterparts. Chapter 13 outlines concrete steps that should be taken in both areas. But the most important first step in changing American attitudes toward Africa, and hence U.S. policy, is to show that Africans are already doing much to help themselves.

Both the impulse to ignore Africa and the impulse to save it derive from a belief that Africans are largely hopeless and helpless. Convinced that Africa is a continent of starving babies, corrupt tyrants, and warring tribes, many Americans believe that providing aid to the continent is like pouring it down the proverbial sinkhole. Convinced that Africans lack the ideas and skills necessary to come up with successful economic policies and political frameworks, U.S. officials exaggerate the need for American mediation and tutelage. Both views are misguided. Africans do need assistance, but they are neither hopeless nor helpless. Many Africans are already taking the initiative, attempting to help themselves in a variety of encouraging ways.

While civil society is far less developed in Africa than in the Western industrialized world, it does exist in one form or another all across the continent, and, most important, it is growing rapidly. One indicator of this trend is the rapid increase in the number of African voluntary organizations that has occurred in recent years.[4] For example, Alan Durning has estimated that in 1984 more than 16,000 local women's groups were operating in Kenya alone; by 1988, this number had increased to 25,000. He also noted that "after Zimbabwe's transfer to black rule in 1980, a similar explosion in community organizing took place there as thousands of women's community gardens and informal small-farmer associations emerged."[5]

The activities of Africa's ubiquitous churches provide another indicator of the growing vitality of civil society. According to Goran Hyden, a leading expert on Africans NGOs, churches "have expanded their activities to include not only education and health, but also support of women's groups, environmental protection, agricultural productivity and a whole range of related development issues affecting groups of rural or urban-based poor people."[6] In many African countries—for example, Kenya, Mozambique, South Africa, Sudan, and Zaire—church leaders have spoken out in defense of the rights of civil society and taken concrete steps to strengthen it. A few of these religious leaders, such as Archbishop Desmond Tutu of South Africa, are well known in the United States; most, such as Bishop Paride Tabane, a courageous and imaginative Catholic bishop in wartorn southern Sudan, are not.

The expansion of civil society has been particularly evident in South Africa.[7] In the 1970s and 1980s, a host of alternative organizations sprang up to challenge the apartheid state's control over the daily life of black South Africans. These included trade unions, sports leagues, weekly newspapers, youth groups, professional and civic associations, women's federations, educational groups, think tanks, and cultural committees. In Ethiopia, the international effort to prevent a repetition of the disastrous famine of 1984–85 has spawned a vast relief network staffed largely by Ethiopians. For example, Catholic Relief Services, one of the largest U.S. organizations in the country, now has 130 employees, all but two of whom are Ethiopian. In addition, the Tigrean People's Liberation Front, which leads the new ruling coalition in Ethiopia, and the Eritrean People's Liberation Front, which now controls Eritrea, established highly effective indigenous relief agencies during the war against the central government.

Across the continent, Africans are now taking deliberate steps to strengthen civil society. In February 1990, a conference on popular participation in Africa, organized by the Economic Commission for Africa (ECA), was held in Tanzania. A diverse range of participants, including almost two hundred representatives of African voluntary organizations from almost every country of Africa, attended. Out of this meeting came the "African Charter for Popular Participation in Development and Transformation," calling for "an opening up of [the] political process to accommodate freedom of opinions, tolerate differences, accept consensus on issues as well as ensure the effective participation of the people and their organizations and associations."[8]

One recent example of efforts by Africans to help themselves is the development of FOVAD (Forum des Organisations Volontaires Africaines de Développement), an Africa-based umbrella organization created to foster links among voluntary development organizations run by Africans. In 1988–89, FOVAD and InterAction organized a series of meetings aimed at strengthening and balancing the partnership among American and African NGOs.[9] Yet another potentially significant initiative is the Africa Leadership Forum, a private organization formed by General Olusegun Obasanjo, the former president of Nigeria. The Forum has brought together African leaders for meetings on a wide variety of economic and political issues. Its major priority is to establish a Conference on Security, Stability, Development and Cooperation in Africa. Inspired by the Conference on Security and Cooperation in Europe (CSCE), this effort represents a serious attempt to develop a new set of norms and strategies for the continent. One encouraging aspect of this initiative is the success it has already achieved in creating a dialogue among African elites about their responsibility for the continent's problems.

These diverse efforts by Africans to confront the continent's problems and gain control of their lives all need to be publicized, encouraged, and supported. They are the best hope for a more democratic, just, prosperous, and stable Africa. Until American policymakers recognize this reality, U.S. policy will continue to produce dismal returns.

13

A NEW U.S. POLICY TOWARD AFRICA

Despite the changing realities described in the preceding chapters, the main debate over U.S. policy toward Africa continues to center on finding new ways to get Washington to devote more attention and resources to the continent. Members of Congress and the various domestic constituencies still use most of their energy to exert pressure on the executive branch to act, rather than seeking to find ways to do things themselves independently of the U.S. government. But more U.S. aid and increased executive branch involvement with African issues are not the answer to Africa's problems. Instead, policies that will limit the damage U.S. officials can do to the continent and help to mobilize America's "third sector" to provide greater assistance to African civil society are needed.

DOING NO HARM

An important first step toward creating a more positive and productive relationship between the United States and Africa would be for the U.S. Congress to establish strong, clear, and consistent limits on official involvement in Africa. To begin with, a simpler and more coherent set of rules should replace the existing maze of congressionally imposed rules restricting foreign aid. Those rules should include the following:

- The United States shall not aid any government that does not guarantee its citizens basic civil liberties, including freedom of speech, freedom of association, and due process of law. In countries where basic civil liberties are not guaranteed, all official U.S. assistance must be channeled through independent nongovernmental organizations.
- The United States government shall not provide any military assistance to either African governments or opposition movements.

117

- The United States government shall not provide any assistance to political candidates or parties in Africa.

- No less than 50 percent of all official U.S. aid to Africa must be channeled through U.S. nongovernmental organizations.

With the end of the Cold War, the United States no longer has any substantial geopolitical interests that require military or political intervention in Africa. The outcome of the many ongoing struggles for political supremacy in Africa will not threaten the security or welfare of the United States. (I may prefer Nelson Mandela to Chief Buthelezi in South Africa, or Amos Sawyer to Charles Taylor in Liberia, or John Garang to Mohamed Beshir in Sudan, or Joaquim Chissano to Afonso Dhlakama in Mozambique, but I strongly doubt that U.S. national interests will be much affected over the long run by which, if any, of these leaders eventually triumph.)

Adopting the above guidelines would greatly limit the ability of U.S. officials to influence and shape political developments on the continent. Thus, Washington could not continue to provide assistance to rulers like Zaire's Mobutu, Malawi's Banda, or Kenya's Moi. It would have to drop plans to help Nelson Mandela and the ANC organize a political party in South Africa, but it would also be barred from aiding Chief Buthelezi and his Inkatha Freedom party. The United States would not be able to buy the UN votes of African dictators with promises of diplomatic and economic support. Individuals and private groups in the United States would be free to support whomever they wished as long as they did not use U.S. taxpayers' dollars to do so.

Along with these guidelines, Congress should create a review process that would encourage informed public debate over U.S. involvement on the continent and ensure that the guidelines are followed. As part of the annual appropriations process, Congress should require the president to submit a country-by-country report on each aid recipient's record in guaranteeing basic civil liberties and the effectiveness of U.S. nongovernmental organizations in strengthening indigenous institutions. This report would replace the existing human rights report and other foreign aid reports Congress now requires. Each year, Congress should hold hearings to allow interested individuals and organizations to critique the administration's findings. This would ensure greater official accountability and make it less likely that midlevel officials, who serve as the primary day-to-day link between Washington and Africa, could establish cozy relationships with African governments. Replacing existing legislation with the guidelines and process just outlined also would give U.S. Africa policy some much-needed coherence.

The positive effects of a policy of principled nonintervention would more than outweigh any short-term costs, such as having some African governments vote against U.S. initiatives at the United Nations. Washington would no longer be dragged into obscure political quarrels in small, out-of-the-way places with names most Americans cannot even pronounce. And such an approach would cost American taxpayers very little in additional aid funds.

MOBILIZING AMERICA'S THIRD SECTOR

The primary goal of U.S. policy should be to expand and deepen contacts between America's third sector and African civil society. This would facilitate the development of a diverse network of personal and institutional linkages that would empower Africans and heighten the interest of important American constituencies in Africa. A strategy to achieve this goal should consider several points.

First, a great many associations and institutions in the United States already have ties with Africa. Many more groups would like to develop such ties, but lack the knowledge and resources necessary to do so.

Second, no group or institution has a monopoly on wisdom about Africa, or an exclusive right to organize contacts between Africans and Americans. To the contrary, the more diverse and numerous the individuals and institutions that are drawn into relationships with Africa, the better.

Third, the strongest and most enduring ties between Africans and Americans are those based on common personal and professional commitments and interests. Emphasis needs to be placed on interchange between churches; labor unions; professional associations; and groups with common causes—AIDS prevention, wildlife preservation, human rights, and the like.

Finally, approaches to building deep and lasting personal ties must take full advantage of the vast size and geographical diversity of the United States. New York and Washington are not necessarily the best places for Africans to visit. The multiplier effect of personal contacts in places off the beaten track, such as Cedar Rapids and San Francisco, is surprisingly high. People there seem to attach a higher value to international contacts than do Eastern insiders, who are besieged by a constant flow of visitors.

The three most important practical steps that could be taken to enhance the ability of America's third sector to develop linkages with Africa are the following:

- Establish a clearinghouse and coordinating office in Washington to collect and disseminate information about African visitors, programs around the country dealing with Africa, and individuals and groups in the United States interested in establishing contacts with Africans. A possible model for such an organization is the Citizens Democracy Project that was established at the direction of President Bush in 1990 to create links between Americans and Eastern Europeans;

- Create a network of regional African societies in key cities around the country to stimulate local interest in Africa, host African visitors, and promote exchange visits between the United States and Africa;

- Create a grants program to enable private American institutions and associations to establish and maintain linkages with African counterparts;

- Set aside 10 percent of all U.S. aid funds to Africa to fund these programs.

Effective national organizations concerned with Africa already exist. The most significant of these, the African-American Institute (AAI) and TransAfrica, have done a great deal to promote interest in Africa and continue to play a vital role. But they cannot bear the entire burden of improving U.S. relations with Africa. AAI focuses most of its public outreach effort on educating and informing elite opinion in Washington and New York. TransAfrica directs its efforts at building an African-American constituency for Africa. For both organizations, influencing official Washington is a primary concern, and both relate more to governments and political parties than to civil society. Although they are developing plans for greater outreach efforts, neither has yet established a strong ongoing presence outside of Washington and New York.

Regional organizations concerned with international affairs—for example, the Southern Center for International Affairs, the Chicago Council on Foreign Relations, and the Los Angeles World Affairs Council—devote relatively little attention to Africa. When they do host discussions on Africa, the topic is usually South Africa and the speaker is more often than not a government official or high-profile figure, such as Archbishop Desmond Tutu. Most of the leaders of these organizations express interest in doing more on Africa but believe that most of their members are not interested in African issues, and the fact that no one is providing resources to develop interest in Africa deters them from doing more. By contrast, money is available—much of it provided by foreign governments and organizations, and the American business community—to promote interest in (and exchanges with) Germany, Japan, Mexico, and a host of other countries. But because of the endemic poverty of African governments and the lack of significant U.S. business interests in Africa, money is not available specifically for African programs.

Neither the existing national organizations concerned with Africa nor the regional organizations concerned with international affairs are likely to become effective catalysts for successful regional initiatives. Doing so would require them to alter their basic modus operandi in too many ways. What is needed instead is a national clearinghouse and a network of regional African societies led by individuals who are enthusiastic about Africa and knowledgeable about America's third sector. The primary functions of the new regional institutions should be to identify groups with a potential interest in or connection with Africa; to sponsor and coordinate visits by Africans to their region; to organize exchange visits to Africa; to serve as a resource for schools, churches, civic groups, and others interested in learning about Africa; and to pass along information to the national clearinghouse. A national clearinghouse also could foster a symbiotic relationship among regional African societies, national organizations concerned with Africa, and regional international affairs groups that would benefit all three sets of institutions. Regional African societies could provide national organizations with a better means of reaching out to constituencies across the country. National organizations, with their access to high-visibility speakers, would be an invaluable resource for regional societies. Similarly, regional African societies could assist their counterparts concerned with international affairs generally in developing African programs and increasing interest in Africa.

Creating regional African societies would require a substantial commitment of financial and organizational resources. Once established, however, such societies could draw on many assets that are currently being squandered. One underutilized asset is the hundreds of thousands of Africans who are resident in the United States along with the large number of African graduates of American universities and colleges. These individuals provide a natural building block for societal linkages. Most of them are articulate, well educated, and deeply concerned about developments in their home countries. With few exceptions, however, efforts to involve them in building links with Africa have been meager.

The visitor programs sponsored by the U.S. government, especially the U.S. Information Agency (USIA) international visitor program, are a second underutilized asset. African visitors are farmed out to several agencies that specialize in programming foreign visitors. Individual programs tend to be ad hoc and uneven. Little effort is made to create lasting ties between the visitors and their American contacts. These visitors represent a squandered resource that could be put to much better use, especially if the USIA officers in Africa who are responsible for selecting visitors worked with a national clearinghouse and made the development of society-to-society relations a major criterion in the selection process and if regional African societies were themselves responsible for most of the programming.

One example of the potential impact regional African initiatives could have is the Africa Focus Project, created in early 1988 by the United Nations Non-Governmental Liaison Service in cooperation with the international division of the YMCA. The main object of this initiative was to focus attention on Africa's economic crisis. As of 1990, eleven U.S. cities were participating in the project. One of the most successful projects was conducted in San Francisco in April 1990 and April 1991. Despite extremely limited core resources, the organizers promoted a wide range of educational, cultural, and other events at a number of different institutions including business groups, community organizations, schools, and universities.

Another helpful measure would be to encourage universities, private voluntary organizations, and other groups to establish more ties with African counterparts. Putting more Americans in direct contact with Africans would do much to dispel negative perceptions of the continent. Americans would learn that as bad as conditions are in Africa, the vast majority of Africans are not backward natives, helpless victims, or ruthless thugs. They are humble, hardworking individuals struggling in the face of tremendous obstacles to build a better life for themselves and their families.

Creating practical ties—as opposed to ideological and romantic bonds—between Americans and Africans also would foster a transfer of knowledge and skills much more effectively and lastingly than any official technical assistance program can. Given the technological revolutions that have occurred in transportation, communications, and computers, human links once established can be maintained on an almost daily basis over thousands of miles.

Finally, increasing contacts between America's third sector and African civil society would be the most effective means of promoting human rights and democracy in Africa. Such contacts can help to provide Africans with the wherewithal to survive and resist government repression. Just as important, they constrain the oppressors by raising the international costs of oppression. It is much easier to silence, jail, torture, and murder nameless individuals and groups than it is to victimize those who have through personal and professional contacts become part of a community that transcends national boundaries.

Among the efforts already underway to link America's third sector with Africa are:

- An effort by the American Association for the Advancement of Science to link American scientific and engineering societies with those in Africa;

- A human rights internship program organized by the Institute of International Education that places human rights activists from Africa in internships with U.S. human rights groups;

- Journalism fellowship programs such as the one sponsored by the Alfred Friendly Foundation that allow African journalists to spend a year working on the staff of an American newspaper.

Lobbying the U.S. government, private foundations, and other groups to commit more resources to programs such as these will yield far higher returns over the long term than increasing the proportion of official development assistance funds committed to Africa.

These are modest proposals. They will not capture many newspaper headlines. But they could, if adequately funded and sustained, make a significant difference in the way Americans relate to Africa, and they would help Africans to help themselves in concrete ways.

NOTES

CHAPTER 1

1. Jo Thomas, "Gorbachev Starts a Visit to Britain with Soviet Group," *New York Times,* December 16, 1984, p. 1.
2. On the impact of the end of the Cold War on Africa, see Michael Clough, "Africa in the 1990s," *CSIS Africa Notes,* no. 107 (1990); Martin Lowenkopf, "If the Cold War Is Over Will the United States Still Care?" *CSIS Africa Notes,* no. 98 (1989); David Newsom, "After the Cold War: U.S. Interest in Sub-Sahara Africa," *Washington Quarterly,* vol. 13, no. 1 (Winter 1990), pp. 99–113; Richard Barnet, "But What About Africa?" *Harpers,* May 1990, pp. 43–51; Ray Bonner, "African Democracy," *The New Yorker,* September 3, 1990, pp. 93–105; and R. Stephen Brent, "Aiding Africa," *Foreign Policy,* no. 80 (Winter 1990–91): 121–40.

CHAPTER 2

1. The best histories of early U.S. policy toward Africa are Waldemar Nielson, *The Great Powers and Africa* (New York: Praeger, 1969); and Vernon McKay, *Africa in World Politics* (New York: Harper & Row, 1963). Useful overviews are provided in Sanford J. Ungar, *Africa: The People and Politics of an Emerging Continent* (New York: Simon and Schuster, 1985), pp. 37–84; and Helen Kitchen, "Still on Safari," in L. Carl Brown, ed., *Centerstage: American Diplomacy since World War Two* (New York: Holmes and Meier, 1990), pp. 171–92.
2. Henry A. Byroade, "The World's Colonies and Ex-Colonies: A Challenge to America," *Department of State Bulletin* 29, no. 751 (November 16, 1953): 656.
3. Mason Sears, *Years of High Purpose: From Trusteeship to Nationhood* (Washington, D.C.: University Press of America, 1980), p. 13.
4. Byroade, "The World's Colonies and Ex-Colonies," p. 656.
5. "The Vice-President's Report to the President on His Trip to Africa, February 28–March 21, 1957," April 5, 1957, White House Office Files, Dwight D. Eisenhower Presidential Library.
6. See Richard Mahoney, *JFK: Ordeal in Africa* (New York: Oxford University Press, 1983).
7. Arthur Schlesinger, *A Thousand Days* (Boston: Houghton Mifflin Company, 1965), p. 552.
8. Ibid., p. 554.
9. Arnold Rivkin, "Lost Goals in Africa," *Foreign Affairs* 44, no. 1 (October 1965): 113.
10. George Ball, *The Discipline of Power* (New York: Little, Brown & Co., 1968), p. 234.

11. Anthony Lake, *The "Tar Baby" Option: American Policy Toward Southern Rhodesia* (New York: Columbia University Press, 1976), p. 75.

12. Quoted in Roger Morris, *Uncertain Greatness: Henry Kissinger and American Foreign Policy* (New York: Harper & Row, 1977), p. 17.

13. "U.S. Foreign Policy for the 1970s: A New Strategy for Peace," Report to the Congress by Richard Nixon, President of the United States, February 18, 1970 (Washington, D.C.: Government Printing Office), p. 84.

14. "U.S. Foreign Policy for the 1970s: The Emerging Structure of Peace," Report to the Congress by Richard Nixon, President of the United States, February 9, 1972 (Washington, D.C.: Government Printing Office), p. 104.

15. For the text of NSSM 39, see Mohamed El-Khawas, *NSSM 39: The Kissinger Study of Southern Africa* (Westport CT: Lawrence Hill and Co., 1976). For background on NSSM 39, see Lake, *The "Tar Baby" Option*, pp. 123–47; and Morris, *Uncertain Greatness*, pp. 107–20.

16. On the history of the Angolan conflict, see John Marcum, *The Angolan Revolution*, vols. 1 and 2 (Cambridge, MA: MIT, 1969, 1978).

17. "U.S. Involvement in Civil War in Angola," Hearings, Subcommittee on African Affairs, Committee on Foreign Relations, United States Senate, 94th Congress, 2d Session, January 29, February 3–4 and 6, 1976, p. 16.

18. Ibid., p. 15.

19. The most useful analyses of the U.S. decision to intervene in Angola are Roger Morris, "The Proxy War in Angola," *The New Republic*, January 31, 1976, pp. 19–23; Nathaniel Davis, "The Angola Decision of 1975: A Personal Memoir," *Foreign Affairs* 57, no. 1 (Fall 1978): 109–24; John Stockwell, *In Search of Enemies: A CIA Story*, (New York: W.W. Norton, 1978); and William Hyland, *Mortal Rivals* (New York: Random House, 1987), pp. 130–47.

20. On Soviet intervention in Africa and the Third World in the 1970s, see Bruce Porter, *The USSR in Third World Conflicts* (Cambridge: Cambridge University Press, 1984); and Raymond Garthoff, *Détente and Confrontation* (Washington D.C.: Brookings Institution, 1985).

21. Cyrus Vance, *Hard Choices: Critical Years in America's Foreign Policy* (New York: Simon and Schuster, 1983), p. 84.

22. On the Angola-Namibia negotiations, see Gillian Gunn, "A Guide to the Intricacies of the Angola-Namibia Negotiations," *CSIS Africa Notes*, no. 90 (1988); and Michael Clough, "The Superpowers and Southern Africa: From Confrontation to Cooperation," in John de St. Jorre et al., *Changing Fortunes: War, Diplomacy and Economics in Southern Africa* (New York: Foreign Policy Association, forthcoming); Sean McCormack, "Angola: The Road to Peace," *CSIS Africa Notes*, no. 125 (1991).

23. See Winrich Kuhne, "What Does the Case of Mozambique Tell Us About Soviet Ambivalence Toward Africa," *CSIS Africa Notes*, no. 46 (1985).

24. See Elizabeth Valkenier, *The USSR and the Third World: An Economic Bind* (New York: Praeger, 1983); Jerry Hough, *The Struggle for the Third World* (Washington, D.C.: Brookings Institution, 1986); and S. Neil MacFarlane, "The Soviet Union and Southern Africa Security," *Problems of Communism* 38 (March–June 1989): 71–89.

25. For a critique of the Reagan doctrine, see Stephen Van Evera, "The Case Against Intervention," *The Atlantic* (July 1990) pp. 72–74; and Michael

Clough, "Coming to Terms with Radical Socialism," in Michael Clough, ed., *Reassessing the Soviet Challenge in Africa* (Berkeley, CA: Institute of International Studies, 1986), pp. 69–90.

CHAPTER 3

1. Chester Bowles, *Africa's Challenge to America* (Berkeley: University of California Press, 1956), p. 51.
2. "Speaking Out: The African-American Manifesto on Southern Africa," *Ebony* 32, no. 2 (December 1976): 88.
3. Jesse Jackson, "Setting the Policy Agenda," *Africa Report* 33, no. 3 (May–June 1988): 16.
4. Ray Cline, "Africa's Importance in Global Strategy," in Helen Kitchen, ed., *Options for U.S. Policy Toward Africa*, AEI Foreign Policy and Defense Review 1, no. 1 (1979): 10–13.
5. Henry Kissinger, "The United States and Africa: Strengthened Ties for an Era of Change," *Department of State Bulletin* 75, no. 1939 (August 1976): 258.
6. Anthony Lake, "Africa in a Global Perspective," *Department of State Bulletin* 77, no. 2007 (1977): 844.
7. On the strategic minerals debate, see Michael Shafer, "Mineral Myths," *Foreign Policy*, no. 47 (Summer 1982): 154–71.
8. Julian Simon, "The Scarcity of Raw Materials," *The Atlantic* 247, no.6 (June 1981): 33–41.
9. Two important studies challenging the argument that U.S. interests were threatened by radical regimes in the Third World were Robert Price, *U.S. Foreign Policy in Sub-Saharan Africa: National Interest and Global Strategy* (Berkeley, CA: Institute of International Studies, 1978); and Richard Feinberg, *The Intemperate Zone: The Third World Challenge to U.S. Foreign Policy* (New York: W. W. Norton, 1983).
10. Noel Koch, "Some Observations on U.S. Security Interests in Africa," *CSIS Africa Notes*, no. 49 (1985).
11. Andrew Kamarck, "The African Economy and International Trade," in Walter Goldschmidt, ed., *The United States and Africa* (New York: Praeger, 1963), p. 159.

CHAPTER 4

1. James E. Baker, J. Daniel O'Flaherty, and John de St. Jorre, *Public Opinion Poll on American Attitudes Toward South Africa* (New York: Carnegie Endowment for International Peace, 1979), p. 7.
2. On media coverage of Africa, see "Capturing the Continent: U.S. Media Coverage of Africa," *Africa News Special Report* (Durham, NC: Africa News, 1990).
3. Stanford J. Ungar, *Africa: The People and Politics of an Emerging Continent* (New York: Simon and Schuster, 1985), p. 21.

4. Immanuel Wallerstein, *Africa: The Politics of Independence* (New York: Vintage Books, 1971), p. 11.
5. John Hatch, *Africa Emergent* (Chicago: Henry Regnery Co., 1974), p. 5.
6. Some of the harshest assessments of developments on the continent have been provided by journalists; see David Lamb, *The Africans* (New York: Vintage, 1987); and Blaine Hardin, *Africa: Dispatches from a Fragile Continent* (New York: W. W. Norton, 1990). For an account that is more sympathetic to Africa, see Jennifer Whitaker, *How Can Africa Survive?* (New York: Harper & Row, 1988).

CHAPTER 5

1. Rupert Emerson, *Africa and United States Policy* (Englewood Cliffs, NJ: Prentice-Hall, 1967), p. 108.
2. David Newsom, "African Development and U.S. Foreign Policy," *Issue*, no. 3 (Fall 1973): 12.
3. Jane Banfield Haynes, "ASA Meeting Disrupted by Racial Crisis," *Africa Report* (December 1969): 16.
4. Idrian Resnick, "The Future of African Studies After Montreal," *Africa Report* (December 1969): 23.
5. Michael Bratton et al., "How Africanists View U.S. Africa Policy: Results of a Survey," *Issue* (Fall 1991).
6. Emerson, *Africa and U.S. Policy*, p. 52.
7. C. Erik Lincoln, "The Race Problem and International Relations," in George Sheperd, ed., *Racial Influences on American Foreign Policy* (New York: Basic Books, 1970), p. 57.
8. Anthony Lake, *The "Tar Baby" Option: American Policy Toward Southern Rhodesia* (New York: Columbia University Press, 1976), p. 285.
9. Tilden LeMelle, "American Black Constituency and Africa: A Rejoinder," in Rene Lemarchand, ed., *American Policy in Southern Africa* (Washington, D.C.: University Press of America, 1981), pp. 357–74.
10. On the debate among black opinion leaders concerning usage of the term African-American, see Ben L. Martin, "From Negro to Black to African American," *Political Science Quarterly* 106, no. 1 (Spring 1991): 83–108.
11. Alfred Hero, *American Religious Groups View Foreign Policy: Trends in Rank-and-File Opinion, 1937–1969* (Durham, NC: Duke University Press, 1973), p. 389.
12. Ibid., p. 395.
13. James E. Baker, J. Daniel O'Flaherty, and John de St. Jorre, *Public Opinion Poll on American Attitudes Toward South Africa* (New York: Carnegie Endowment for International Peace, 1979), p. 5.
14. *The Gallup Poll Monthly*, no. 293 (February 1990): 2–3.
15. Joint Center for Political Studies, *Africa in the Minds and Deeds of African-American Leaders*, draft report to the Rockefeller Foundation, May 14, 1990.
16. On the history of African-American interest in foreign policy, see Henry Jackson, *From the Congo to Soweto: U.S. Foreign Policy Toward Africa Since 1960*

(New York: Columbia University Press, 1977), pp. 121–68; Herschelle Challenor, "The Influence of Black Americans on U.S. Foreign Policy Toward Africa," in Abdul Aziz Said, ed., *Ethnicity and U.S. Foreign Policy,* (New York: Praeger, 1977), pp. 143–82; and Ronald Walters, "African-American Influence on U.S. Foreign Policy Toward South Africa," in Mohamed Ahrari, ed., *Ethnic Groups and U.S. Foreign Policy* (Greenwood, CT: Greenwood Press, 1987), pp. 65–82.

17. Quoted in Jackson, *From the Congo to Soweto,* pp. 145–46.
18. Memo to McGeorge Bundy from R.W. Komer and Rick Haynes, March 30, 1965, National Security Council files, Lyndon Baines Johnson Presidential Library.
19. "Democratic Presidential Candidates Address Black Foreign Policy Concerns," *TransAfrica Forum Issue Brief* (June–July): 1983.
20. "Take Part in History," flyer announcing the first African–African-American summit, undated.
21. See Donald McHenry, "Captive of No Group," *Foreign Policy,* no. 15 (Summer 1974): 142–49.
22. See InterAction, *Member Profiles* (New York: InterAction, May 1989).
23. See Lars Schoutz, *Human Rights and U.S. Policy Toward Latin America* (Princeton, NJ: Princeton University Press, 1981).
24. See Nomsa Daniels, *Protecting the African Environment: Reconciling North-South Perspectives.* (New York: Council on Foreign Relations, forthcoming).
25. See Raymond Arsenault, "White on Chrome: Southern Congressmen and Rhodesia, 1962–1971," *Issue* 2, no. 4 (Winter 1972): 46–57.
26. Ungar, *Africa,* p. 20.

CHAPTER 6

1. For an excellent portrait of the post–World War II foreign policy establishment, see Walter Issacson and Evan Thomas, *The Wise Men: Six Friends and the World They Shaped* (New York: Simon and Schuster, 1987). See also Geoffrey Hodgson, "The Establishment," *Foreign Policy,* no. 10 (Spring 1973): 3–40.
2. On American's early contacts with Africa, see Edward McKinley, *The Lure of Africa: American Interests in Tropical Africa, 1919–39* (New York: Bobbs-Merrill Co., 1974).
3. *United Nations Statistical Yearbook 1961* (New York: United Nations, 1961), p. 382.
4. Membership Department, Council on Foreign Relations, New York, New York.
5. Office of the Administrator-General, Department of State, Washington, D.C.
6. See Michael Clough, "Beyond Constructive Engagement," *Foreign Policy,* no. 61 (Winter 1985–86): 3–24.
7. Anthony Lake, *The "Tar Baby" Option: American Policy, Toward Southern Rhodesia* (New York: Columbia University Press, 1976), p. 282.
8. On the breakdown of the Cold War consensus, see I. M. Destler et al., *Our Own Worst Enemy* (New York: Simon and Schuster, 1984).

9. See Burdett Loomis, *The New American Politician: Ambition, Entrepreneurship, and the Changing Face of Political Life* (New York: Basic Books, 1988).
10. Roger Morris, *Uncertain Greatness: Henry Kissinger and American Foreign Policy* (New York: Harper & Row, 1977), p. 42.
11. Michael J. Robinson, "Three Faces of Congressional Media," in Thomas E. Mann and Norman J. Ornstein, eds., *The New Congress* (Washington, D.C.: Congressional Quarterly, 1981), p. 83.
12. Ibid., p. 64.
13. See Carol Lancaster, "The New Politics of U.S. Aid to Africa," *CSIS Africa Notes,* no. 120 (1991): 2.

CHAPTER 7

1. "Department of Defense Appropriations for 1991," Hearings, Subcommittee on the Department of Defense, Committee on Appropriations, House of Representatives, 101st Congress, 2d Session, February 8, 1990, p. 15.
2. "Authorization Request for Foreign Assistance, the Department of State, and USIA for Fiscal Years 1990–91," Hearings, Committee on Foreign Affairs, House of Representatives, 101st Congress, 2d Session, February 22, March 1 and 6, 1990, Washington D.C., p. 131.
3. "Prepared Statement of Secretary of Defense Dick Cheney to the Senate Armed Services Committee, February 21, 1991," *Defense Issues* 6, no.6 (1991): 4.
4. Department of Defense Appropriations, Fiscal Year 1991, Hearings, Committee on Appropriations, U.S. Senate, 101st Congress, 2d Session, 1990, p. 262.
5. "The Gulf: A World United Against Aggression," *U.S. Department of State Dispatch* 1, no. 14 (December 3, 1990): 295.
6. "The UN: World Parliament of Peace," *US Department of State Dispatch* 1, no. 6 (October 8, 1990): 151.
7. For the text see, *New York Times,* January 30, 1991, p. A12.
8. "Foreign Policy Priorities," hearings, Foreign Relations Committee, U.S. Senate, 101st Congress, 1st Session, February 2, 1990, p. 24.
9. "The 1990 Houston Economic Summit," *Foreign Policy Bulletin* 1, no. 2 (September/October 1990): p. 56.
10. Ben J. Wattenberg, *The First Universal Nation* (New York: Free Press, 1990), p. 196.
11. Ibid., p. 201.
12. See Francis Fukuyama, "The End of History," *The National Interest,* no. 16 (Summer 1989).
13. Joshua Muravchik, *Exporting Democracy: Fulfilling America's Destiny* (Washington, D.C.: American Enterprise Institute, 1991).
14. Olé R. Holsti and James N. Rosenau, "The Emerging U.S. Consensus on Foreign Policy," *Orbis* 34, no. 4 (Fall 1990): p. 583.
15. John E. Reilly, *American Public Opinion and U.S. Foreign Policy 1991* (Chicago: Chicago Council on Foreign Relations, 1991), p. 15.

16. "The Democracy Initiative," U.S. Agency for International Development, Washington, D.C., December 1990, p. i.
17. "Democratic Change in Africa," *U.S. Department of State Dispatch* 1, no. 12 (November 19, 1990): 272.
18. Ibid., p. 273.
19. Jonas Savimbi, "Democracy in Africa," *Freedom at Issue* (November–December 1990): 31.
20. Richard Barnet, "After the Cold War," *The New Yorker*, January 1, 1990, p. 76.
21. John Sewell, "The Metamorphosis of the Third World: U.S. Interests in the 1990s," in William Brock and Robert Hormats, eds., *The Global Economy: America's Role in the Decade Ahead* (New York: W. W. Norton, 1990), pp.120–46.
22. "Compact for African Development," in Robert J. Berg and Jennifer Seymour Whitaker, eds., *Strategies for African Development* (Berkeley, CA: University of California Press, 1986), p. 562.
23. Reilly, *American Public Opinion and U.S. Foreign Policy,* p. 15.
24. Ibid., p. 29.
25. Christine Contee, "What Americans Think: Views on Development and U.S. Third World Relations" (Washington, D.C.: Overseas Development Council, 1986).
26. Patrick Buchanan, "America First—And Second, and Third," *The National Interest*, no. 19 (Spring 1990): 77–82.
27. Stephen Van Evera, *Wars of Intervention: Why They Shouldn't Have a Future, Why They Do*, CCS Policy Report, no. 3 (Cambridge, MA: Committee on Common Security, June 1990), p. 21.

CHAPTER 8

1. See Paul Kennedy, *The Rise and Fall of the Great Powers* (New York: Vintage Books, 1989); and David Calleo, *Beyond American Hegemony* (New York: Basic Books, 1987).
2. Joseph Nye, *Bound to Lead* (New York: Basic Books, 1990), pp. 72–73.
3. David Boren, "New Decade, New World, New Strategy," *Washington Post*, January 2, 1990.
4. "A New Balance of Power," *New York Times*, July 12, 1990, p. 1.
5. Shafiqul Islam, *Yen For Development* (New York: Council on Foreign Relations, 1991), pp. 219–222.

CHAPTER 9

1. Alan Durning, "People Power and Development," *Foreign Policy*, no. 76 (Fall 1989): 66–67.
2. Ben J. Wattenberg, *The First Universal Nation* (New York: Free Press, 1990), p. 9.
3. "America's Hottest Export: Pop Culture," *Fortune*, December 31, 1990, pp. 50–60.

4. Alexis de Tocqueville, *Democracy in America*, vol. 2, (Toronto: Vintage Books, 1945), p. 123.
5. Peter Drucker, *New Realities* (New York: HarperCollins, 1989) p. 196.
6. Ibid., p. 199.
7. Michael O'Neill, *The Third America* (San Francisco: Jossey-Bass, 1990), pp. 1–2.
8. Agency for International Development, *Development and the National Interest: U.S. Economic Assistance into the 21st Century* (Washington, D.C.: February 1989).
9. O'Neill, *The Third America*, p. 124.
10. Medea Benjamin and Andrea Freedman, *Bridging the Global Gap* (Cabin John, MD: Seven Locks Press, 1989).
11. Michael Shuman, "Dateline Main Street: Local Foreign Policy," *Foreign Policy*, no. 65 (Winter 1986–87): 154.
12. Brian O'Connell and Ann Brown O'Connell, *Volunteers in Action* (New York: The Foundation Center, 1989), p.1.
13. *The Foundation Directory*, 1991 ed. (New York: The Foundation Center, 1990), p. vi.
14. Susan Strange, *Markets and States* (New York: Basil Blackwell, 1988), p. 133.
15. John Naisbitt and Patricia Aburndene, *Megatrends 2000* (New York: William Morrow & Co., 1990), p. 141.

CHAPTER 10

1. "Political and Economic Situation in Zaire—Fall 1981," Hearings before the Subcommittee on Africa, Committee on Foreign Affairs, House of Representatives, 97th Congress, 1st session, September 15, 1981, p. 4.
2. Henry Kissinger, *Department of State Bulletin* 74, no. 1926 (May 31, 1976): 702.
3. *Department of State Bulletin*, 89, no. 2151 (October 1989): 15–16.
4. Lawyers Committee for Human Rights, *Zaire: Repression as Policy* (New York: Lawyers Committee for Human Rights, 1990), p. 192.
5. Committee on Foreign Relations, U.S. Senate, *Zaire: A Staff Report* (Washington D.C.: Government Printing Office, 1982) p. 11.
6. Lawyers Committee for Human Rights, *Zaire*, p. 8.
7. Frank Wisner, Deputy Assistant Secretary of State for Africa, *Department of State Bulletin* 85, no. 2098 (May 1985): 50.
8. "President Carter's News Conference of April 22," *Department of State Bulletin* 76, no. 1977 (May 16, 1977): 482.
9. Richard Moose, "U.S. Policy Toward Zaire," *Department of State Bulletin* 79, no. 2026 (May 1979): 42–45.
10. Jonathan Randall, "Return of Exiled Rival Bolsters Position of Sudan's Ruler," *Washington Post*, April 11, 1978, p. A17.
11. "Breadbasket? Sudanese Agricultural Development Plan," *Forbes*, August 1, 1976, p. 56.
12. "Another African Country Turns From Russia to the U.S.," *U.S. News and World Report*, September 26, 1977, p. 76.

13. Ann Mosely Lesch, "A View From Khartoum," *Foreign Affairs* 65, no. 4 (Summer 1987): 810.

14. U.S. Congress. House. Committee on Foreign Relations. Subcommittee on Africa. Crocket testimony, "Foreign Assistance Legislation for Fiscal Years 1984–85," Part 8. 98th Cong. 1st sess. Mar.–Apr. 1983.

15. "U.S. Arms Aid to Sudan Likely to Face Delays," *Wall Street Journal*, October 14, 1981, p. 4.

16. Phillip Shabacoff, "U.S. Stops Helping Sudan's Economy," *New York Times*, February 18, 1985, p. A1.

17. "U.S. Releasing $67 Million for Sudan," *New York Times*, April 12, 1985, Section I, p. 8.

18. Richard Moose, "U.S. Policy Toward Liberia," *Department of State Bulletin* 80, no. 2045 (December 1980): 26.

19. Ibid.

20. "U.S. Calls Maneuvers with Liberia a Move to Stabilize Its Regime," *New York Times*, April 5, 1981, p. 10.

21. Leon Dash, "Liberia Executes 5 Members of Ruling Council," *Washington Post*, August 15, 1981, p. A17.

22. "Doe's Harsh Rule Daunts Liberians," *Washington Post*, August 25, 1981, p. A14.

23. William Swing, "Liberia: The Road to Recovery," Current Policy no. 343, Bureau of Public Affairs, U.S. Department of State, Washington, D.C., October 28, 1981, p. 5.

24. Written response to questions, "Foreign Assistance and Related Programs Appropriations for 1984: Africa and Sahel," Hearings, Subcommittee on Foreign Operations, Committee on Appropriations, House of Representatives, 98th Congress, April 28, 1983, p. 445.

25. See Stanley O. Day, "The Liberian Coup, and Others, Seen Through 'Bifocals,'" *New York Times*, April 2, 1981, p. 27; Leon Dash, "Liberians Question Whether Doe Will Return Power to Civilians," *Washington Post*, April 30, 1983, p. A2; and Peter V. Emerson and Joey Shawcross, "Liberia's Democratic Hopes Caught Underfoot of Doe," *Wall Street Journal*, May 28, 1985, p. 31.

26. "Liberia and United States Policy," Hearing, Subcommittee on African Affairs, Committee on Foreign Relations, U.S. Senate, 99th Congress, 1st Session, December 10, 1985, p. 2.

27. "Shultz Sees Liberian Doe, Cites 'Genuine Progress,'" *Washington Post*, January 15, 1987, p. A31.

28. "17 AID Officials to Manage Overhaul of Liberian Finances," *Washington Post*, March 4, 1987, p. A22; "U.S. Will Oversee Liberian Finances," *New York Times*, April 26, 1987, Section I, p. 11; and "Liberia in Grip of Graft, Puts Americans at Treasury's Helm," *Washington Post*, May 29, 1988, p. A29.

29. "Mission to Liberia Evidently Fails," *New York Times*, December 5, 1988, Section IV, p. 6.

30. "U.S. Explains Reluctance to Intervene," *Washington Post*, July 31, 1990, p. A18.

31. Transcript, *MacNeil–Lehrer NewsHour*, June 8, 1990.

32. "While Samuel Doe was still in power, we urged him to move up the date of the next presidential election so that the insurgents could feel that their

grievances could be addressed. You will recall that Samuel Doe had agreed to an election within one year—or mid-1991—and had also agreed not to run for reelection. Unfortunately, these concessions were insufficient for the national patriotic front, which demanded Doe's immediate resignation and exile." Herman Cohen, *U.S. Department of State Dispatch* 1, no. 14 (December 3, 1990): 305.

33. Alison Rosenberg, "FY 1990 Assistance Request for Sub-Saharan Africa," *Department of State Bulletin* 89, no. 2146 (July 1989): 41.

34. Kenneth Brown, "Human Rights Issues in Africa," *Department of State Bulletin* 89, no. 2146 (May 1989): 31.

35. "Department of Defense Appropriations, Fiscal Year 1991," Hearings, Committee on Appropriations, U.S. Senate, 101st Congress, 2d Session, p. 151.

36. Human Rights Watch, *World Report 1990* (New York: Human Rights Watch, 1991), p. 42.

37. "350 Libyans Trained to Oust Qadafi Are to Come to U.S.," *New York Times*, May 17, 1991.

CHAPTER 11

1. See U.S. General Accounting Office, The United States' Response to the Ethiopian Food Crisis (Washington, D.C.: U.S. General Accounting Office, April 8, 1985).

2. "Emergency Assistance to Africa," Joint Hearings, Committee on Foreign Affairs and Select Committee on Hunger, House of Representatives, 98th Congress, 2d Session, September 13, 1984, pp. 78–79.

3. "Food Assistance to Ethiopia," *Department of State Bulletin* 85, no. 2094 (January 1985): 7.

4. "African Hunger Relief Initiative Announced," *Department of State Bulletin* 85, no. 2096 (March 1985): 27.

5. Chester Crocker, "U.S. Assistance and Africa's Economic Crisis," *Department of State Bulletin* 85, no. 2096 (March 1985): 23.

6. Office of the Historian, Bureau of Public Affairs, U.S. Department of State, *The United States and South Africa: U.S. Public Statements and Related Documents, 1977–1985* (Washington, D.C.: U.S. Department of State, September 1985), pp. 79, 82.

7. Ibid., p. 82.

8. Ibid., p. 56.

9. Ibid., p. 58.

10. "Joyous Welcome Home for Bishop Tutu," *New York Times*, October 19, 1984, p. A3.

11. See Michael Clough, "Southern Africa: Challenges and Choices," *Foreign Affairs* 66, no. 5 (Summer 1988): 1067–90.

12. President Reagan, "Ending Apartheid in South Africa," *Department of State Bulletin* 86, no. 2114 (September 1986): 1–5.

13. Office of the Historian, *The United States and South Africa*, p. 316.

14. "U.S. Policy Toward South Africa," Hearings, Committee on Foreign Relations, U.S. Senate, 101st Congress, 1st Session, October, 1989, p. 11.

CHAPTER 12

1. The World Bank, *Sub-Saharan Africa: From Crisis to Sustainable Growth* (Washington, D.C.: The World Bank, 1989), pp. 61–62.
2. Robert H. Jackson and Carl G. Rosberg, "Why Africa's Weak States Persist: The Empirical and the Juridical in Statehood," *World Politics* 35, no.1 (1983): 23.
3. P. T. Bauer, *Reality and Rhetoric: Studies in the Economics of Development* (Cambridge, MA: Harvard University Press, 1984), p. 46.
4. See Pearl Robinson, "Transnational NGO's: A New Direction for U.S. Policy, *Issue* 23, no.1 (Winter 1989): 41–46; Naomi Chazan, "Engaging the State: Associational Life in Sub-Saharan Africa," Paper presented at a workshop entitled "State Power and Social Forces: Struggles and Accommodation," University of Texas, Austin, February 1990; Alan Fowler, "New Scrambles for Africa: Non-Governmental Development Organizations and Their Donors in Kenya," *African Rural and Urban Studies* 1, no.1 (Summer 1990); and Willard Johnson and Vivian Johnson, *West African Governments and Voluntary Development Organizations: Priorities for Partnership* (Lanham, MD: University Press of America, 1990).
5. Alan Durning, "People Power and Development," *Foreign Policy* 76 (Fall 1989): 71.
6. Goren Hyden, *No Shortcuts to Progress* (Berkeley: University of California Press, 1983), p. 117.
7. On civil society in South Africa, see Robert Price, *The Apartheid State in Crisis* (New York: Oxford University Press, 1991); Steven Mufson, *Fighting Years* (New York: Beacon Press, 1990).
8. *African Charter for Popular Participation in Development* (Addis Ababa: United Nations Economic Commission for Africa, 1990), p. 3.
9. Africa Partnership Project, *Toward Partnership in Africa* (New York: American Council for Voluntary Action, 1990).

INDEX

AAI (African-American Institute), 122–23
ABC News, 84, 51
Abrams, Elliot, 86
Addis Ababa, 79, 84, 107
Adventist Development and Relief International, 37
Afghanistan, 57
Africa Focus Project, 84, 123–26
Africa Leadership Forum, 84, 116
African–African American summit, 34
African Charter for Popular Participation in Development and Transformation, 117
African Heritage Studies Association, 27, 28
Africanists, 20, 26–29; and the Bush administration, 110; and the foreign policy establishment, 43–48; and pessimism about Africa, 24–25; and promoting democracy, 58–59
Africare, 37
Africa Watch, 36, 101, 102
AFSCME (American Federation of State, County, and Municipal Employees), 110
AID (Agency for International Development), 42, 58, 72, 97, 104
AIDS crisis, 25, 122
Alfred Friendly Association, 126
Algeria, 6, 22
American Association for the Advancement of Science, 126
American Colonization Society, 91
American Committee on Africa, 29
American Council for Voluntary International Action, 36
American Friends Service Committee, 37

American Red Cross, 37
AmeriCare, 37
Amnesty International, 36
ANC (African National Congress), 105,108–9, 111, 120
Angola, 23, 24, 50, 77; civil war in, 12, 48; and the Clark amendment, 52; cost of reconstructing, 84, 111; and efforts to promote democracy, 59; and Mobutu, 80; and the Nixon administration, 9–10; and the Soviet Union, 38; U.S. investments in, 16; and U.S. trade with Africa, 17
Angolan Task Force, 50
ANLCA (American Negro Leadership Conference on Africa), 32–33, 34
Apple, R. W., 63–64
ASA (African Studies Association), 26, 27–28
Asia, 16, 18, 31, 40, 54. *See also* specific countries
Audobon Society, 37

Baker, James, 57
Ball, George, 7
Banda, Hastings, 120
Barnet, Richard, 59–60
Barre, Siad, 77, 78, 79
Bauer, P. T., 115
Belgium, 79–82
Benjamin, Medea, 72
Beshir, Mohamed, 120
Biafra, 51
Blumenthal, Erwin, 87
Borchegrave, Arnaud de, 42
Boren, David, 63
Botswana, 21
Boucher, Richard, 97

Bowles, Chester, 14
Brazil, 16
Bridging the Global Gap (Benjamin and Freedman), 72–73
Britain, 2, 40, 54, 62–63
Brown, Kenneth, 100
Buchanan, Patrick, 61
Bulgaria, 70
Bush, George (Bush administration), 2, 55, 56; and Chad, 12–13; and the Citizens Democracy Project, 122; and Cuba, 48; and Kenya, 101–2; and the Persian Gulf crisis, 56–57; and Somalia, 100; and South Africa, 47–48, 110; and Zaire, 81
Butcher, Goler, 42
Buthelezi, Mangosuthu, 23, 38, 120
Byrd, Harry, 38, 48
Byrd amendment, 38
Byroade, Henry, 5–6

Cal Tech, 28
Callaghy, Thomas, 87
Cameroon, 16
Canada, 54
CARE, 37, 84, 107
Carlucci, Frank, 41
Carnegie Corporation of New York, 74
Carter, Jimmy (Carter administration), 10, 27, 44, 45, 46; appointment of blacks to key posts, 42; and the Carter Doctrine, 11–12; and Liberia, 95; and Nimeri, 90; and Zaire, 80–83, 84
Catholic Relief Services (CRS), 37, 103, 104, 117
Center for Innovative Diplomacy, 73
Central Africa, 22. *See also* specific countries Central Africa, 72
Chad, 12–13
Cheney, Richard, 55, 56
Chernenko, Konstantin, 2
Chicago Council on Foreign Relations, 60, 84, 121

China, 7, 70; and the changing nature of U.S. global power, 62–63; Tiananmen Square massacre, 75
Chissano, Joaquim, 120
Christian Children's Fund, 37
Church World Service, 37
CIA (Central Intelligence Agency), 15; and the Congo, 80; funding of African programs in the 1950s and 1960s, 28
Citizens Democracy Project, 122
Clark amendment, 52
Cline, Ray, 15
CNN (Cable News Network), 69, 70
Cohen, Herman, 46, 47, 48, 58–59, 100, 133n.32; and Kenya, 102; and Liberia, 97; and South Africa, 110; and Zaire, 86
Cold War, 1–3, 5, 29, 42, 75, 119–20; and aid to Ethiopia, 105; and collective security, 56; and Congress, 108; and containing communism, rationale of, 97; and the impulse to ignore Africa, 112; and the independence of Namibia, 12; and instability in the Third World, increases in, 55; and issue-oriented constituencies, 38; post-, international system, 54, 55; and promoting democracy, 57–58, 100; U.S. aid during, 77–81
COMECON (Council for Mutual Economic Assistance), 12
Committee on African Development Strategies, 60
Committee on Foreign Affairs, 87, 90
Committee on Foreign Relations, 99
Communism, 5, 85; collapse of, in Eastern Europe, 76; containment of, 97; and Nixon's first annual report on foreign policy, 8–9; and the Reagan administration, 57; and South Africa, 108. *See also* Marxism
Comoros Islands, 22
Compact for African Development, 60

Comprehensive Anti-Apartheid Act, 33,52, 107, 110
Conference on Security, Stability, Development and Cooperation in Africa, 84, 116
Congo, 7, 41, 80
Congress, 33, 36, 37, 43, 119–21; Ad Hoc Monitoring Group on Southern Africa, 50; and Africanists, 48; black members of, 33, 46, 50–51, 52–53; Congressional Human Rights Caucus, 50; and Ethiopia, 105; increasing importance of, 40, 48–53; and issue-oriented constituencies, 38; and Liberia, 94, 95; and media consciousness, 51; and promoting democracy, 57; Senate Foreign Relations Committee, 81, 96; and South Africa, 106, 107, 108–9, 110; and Zaire, 81, 85, 87, 102
Congress of Berlin, 114
Council on African Affairs, 32
Council on Foreign Relations, 41, 42, 60, 67
Council on Foundations, 72
Cowan, L. Gray, 26–27 Crocker, Chester, 44, 47, 90, 96, 98, 105–6
CSCE (Conference on Security and Cooperation in Europe), 84, 116
C-SPAN, 51
Cuba, 9, 12, 44, 48
Czechoslovakia, 6

Defense Department (United States), 16, 41
Democracy in America (de Tocqueville), 71
Democracy Initiative program, 58, 114
Democratic National Committee, 33–34
Democratic Party, 38
Dhlakama, Alfonso, 120
Diggs, Charles, 32–33, 50
Djibouti, 21
Doe, Samuel, 13, 77, 78, 79, 91–97, 100, 133 n. 32
Drucker, Peter, 71, 115–16

Du Bois, W. E. B., 32
Duignan, Peter, 27, 28
Dukakis, Michael, 42
Dulles, John Foster, 5
Durning, Alan, 70, 116

East Africa, 22, 42. See also specific countries
Eastern Europe, 76
East Germany, 70
Easum, Donald, 45
ECA (Economic Commission for Africa), 115
Economic Policy Initiative, 112
Economic Summit (July 1990), 57
Egypt, 6, 21, 22, 83; and initiatives in the Middle East, 88; and Sudan, 93
Eisenhower, Dwight D., 5, 6, 73, 80
Emerson, Rupert, 26, 29–30
Eritrean People's Liberation Front, 115
Ethiopia, 4, 21, 23, 77–81; and the Bush administration, 56; cost of reconstructing, 111, 112; famine in, 71, 101–3, 107, 109–11, 115; and the foreign policy establishment, 101; and the Soviet Union, 12, 38, 88
Eurocentrism, 9
Europe, 31, 62–63,, 111. See also specific countries
European Community, 22
Evera, Stephen van, 61

Fauntroy, Walter, 105
Firestone Rubber Company, 92
FNLA (Frente Nacional de Libertacao de Angola), 9
Ford, Gerald, 890
Ford Foundation, 74
Foreign Service, 42
Fortune, 70–71
Foundation Center, 74
FOVAD (Forum des Organisations Volontaires Africaines de Development), 115–18
France, 22, 40, 66; and the changing nature of U.S. global power,

62–63; and the global nature of American interest in Africa, 54; and Mobutu, 80
Fredericks, Wayne, 27, 45
Freedman, Andrea, 72

Gabon, 16
Garang, John, 118
General Accounting Office (U.S.), 94–97
Germany, 54, 56, 66, 121
Ghana, 6, 7, 22, 23, 24, 25
Gingrich, Newt, 34, 49, 105
GNP (gross national product), 64, 78
Gorbachev, Mikhail, 2
Grassroots International, 72
Gray, William, 50
Great Britain. See Britain
Greenpeace, 37
Gromyko, Andrei, 2
Guinea, 6, 7

Habitat for Humanity, 72
Habre, Hissene, 13
Haig, Alexander, 44, 104
Hayden, Thomas, 97
Heifer Project, 37
Helen Keller International, 37
Hempstone, Smith, 101–2
Heritage Foundation, 28
Hoover Institution, 97
Horn of Africa, 10, 12, 15, 21–22, 52, 72, 79. See also specific countries
House Appropriations Committee, 99
House Foreign Affairs Committee, 49, 50, 98–101
House Select Committee on Hunger, 52
Hyden, Gordan, 114

IMF (International Monetary Fund), 67, 87, 89
Indian Ocean Islands, 22
Inkatha Freedom Party, 118
Institute of International Education, 126, 124

InterAction, 36, 37, 116
International Design Assistance Commission, 72
International Rescue Committee, 37
International Sister Restaurant Project, 72
International Voluntary Service, 72
Iran, 11
Iraq, 57
Islam, Shafiqul, 67
Islamic law, 87
Israel, 21
Italy, 56, 66
Ivory Coast, 23, 95

Jackson, Jesse, 14, 33
Jackson, Robert, 118
Japan, 14, 15, 21, 63, 121; aid to Africa by, 66; and the attacks that led to World War II, 56; and the global nature of American interest in Africa, 54; postwar reconstruction of, 111; as the world's leading creditor, 66–67
Johnson, Douglas, 89, 93
Johnson, Lyndon, 7, 27, 32; and the Biafran famine, 51; and pessimism about Africa, 24–25
Joint Center for Political Studies, 31–32
Joint Chiefs of Staff, 42, 55

Kamarck, Andrew, 19
Karl-I-Bond, Nguza, 80–83
Kassebaum, Nancy, 105
Kaunda, Kenneth, 23, 24
Kemp, Jack, 34, 105
Kennan, George, 61
Kennedy, John F., 6, 9, 27; appeal of young African leaders to, 24; and the Congo, 80
Kenya, 1, 21–23, 28, 77–81, 98, 118; and the Bush administration, 99; church leaders in, 114–17; congressional debates on, 37; economic performance of, 78; and the Kennedy administration, 24; reductions of aid to, 13; women's groups in, 114

Kenyatta, Jomo, 24
Khrumah, Kwame, 24
Khrushchev, Nikita, 6
King, Martin Luther, Jr., 32
Kinshasa, 80
Kirkpatrick, Jeane, 23
Kissinger, Henry, 9, 15, 45, 81
Klerk, F. W. de, 47, 109
Koch, Noel, 16
Kuwait, 86

Lake, Anthony, 7, 15, 30, 48
Latin America, 16, 18, 31, 40
Lawyers' Committee for Human
    Rights, 36, 81–84, 108
League of Nations, 56
Lebanon, 72
Lelyveld, Joseph, 41
LeMelle, Tilden, 30
Leninism, 15
Lesotho, 21
Liberia, 28, 77–81, 89–97, 96–99,
    118; and the black lobby, 37; and
    the Bush administration, 56; con-
    gressional debates on, 37; cost of
    reconstructing, 111; economic
    performance of, 78; and the
    Soviet Union, 92, 93
Liberian Shipowners Association, 93
Libya, 13, 22, 99, 100; and the
    Bush administration, 57; and
    Liberia, 93; and Nimeri, 87
Liebenow, J. Gus, 97
Lincoln, Erik, 30
Lippman, Walter, 61
Live Aid concert, 71
Los Angeles World Affairs Council,
    121
Luanda, 10, 12
Lugar, Richard, 105
Lutheran World Relief, 37
Lutheran World Services, 107

MacArthur Foundation, 74
McCluhan, Marshall, 51
McHenry, Donald, 42
MacNeil-Lehrer NewsHour, 51
McPherson, M. Peter, 102
Madagascar, 22

Malawi, 21, 22, 118
Mali, 7
Mandela, Nelson, 23, 31, 107, 109,
    118
Marshall Plan, 4, 63
Marxism, 7, 25, 101. *See also* Com-
    munism
Mauritius, 22
Mediterranean Sea, 22
Mengistu, Haile Mariam, 107
Mennonite Central Committee, 37
Mexico, 54, 75,121
Middle East, 22, 62–63
Mobutu, Sese Seko, 13. 79–85, 84,
    85, 89, 100, 118
Mogadishu, 98
Moi, Daniel Arap, 77, 78, 100, 118
Monrovia, 92, 93, 94–97
Moose, Richard, 44, 84, 84, 92
Morgenthau, Hans, 61
Morocco, 6, 22
Morris, Roger, 51
Mozambique, 12, 22, 56, 118;
    church leaders in, 114–17; cost
    of reconstructing, 111
MPLA (Movimento Popular de Lib-
    ertacao de Angola), 9, 10, 12
Munger, Ned, 28
Muslims, 22, 86
Muzorewa, Abel, 38

Namibia, 10, 12, 21, 22, 77
Nasser, Abdel, 6
National Council of Negro Women,
    37
National Security Memorandum, 9
NATO (North Atlantic Treaty Or-
    ganization), 5
Natural Resources Defense Council,
    37
NBC News, 101, 102
Near East, 40
Neo-Realists, 61
New York Times, 41, 89
Newsom, David, 26
Newsweek, 42
NGOs (international nongovernmen-
    tal organizations), 69, 114, 116
Nicaragua, 21, 57

Nigeria, 16, 22,, 116; civil war in, 41, 51; and oil wealth, squandering of, 25; and U.S. trade, 16, 17
Nightline, 51
Nimeri, Jaafar, 77, 78, 79, 83–91, 90–93
Nixon, Richard, 6, 27, 50; first annual report on foreign policy, 87; and pessimism about Africa, 24–25
Nkrumah, Kwame, 23
Nobel Peace Prize, 104
North Africa, 22. See specific countries
North-South relations, 59–60
NSC (National Security Council), 6
Nye, Joseph, 41–42, 63
Nyerere, Julius, 23, 24

OAU (Organization of Africa Unity), 22
Obasanjo, Olusegun, 116
ODA (overseas development assistance), 64
Overseas Development Council, 60
Oxfam, 37

Paris Peace Conference, 113
Peace Corps, 41
Pentagon, 55, 98
People's Redemption Council, 93
Perkins, Edward, 42
Persian Gulf crisis, 56–57, 88, 100
Philippines, 72
Physicians for Human Rights, 73
Plenty USA, 72
Poland, 21
Portugal, 9
Posner, Michael, 97
Powell, Colin, 42, 55, 56
Pretoria, 48

Qadafi, Mu'ammar, 87, 88, 90, 100

Reagan, Ronald (Reagan administration), 2, 10, 12, 44, 49, 89; and Africanists, 45, 46; and the Bush administration, 57; and communism, 106; and the Ethiopian

famine, 101, 102–3; and Liberia, 93; policy of "constructive engagement," 103; and promoting democracy, 57; and South Africa, 103–5, 108, 109; and Sudan, 88–91; and Zaire, 84
Republican Party, 34
Resnick, Idrian, 28
Rhodesia, 10, 21, 38, 48
Robinson, Randall, 33
Rockefeller Foundation, 74
Rosberg, Carl, 113
Rosenberg, Alison, 98
Rumania, 70
Rwanda, 56

SACP (South African Communist Party), 106, 107
Sadat, Anwar, 88
Sadiq al-Mahdi, 86
San Francisco Conference, 113
Saudi Arabia, 86
Save the Children, 37, 101
Savimbi, Jonas, 12, 24, 28, 38, 47–48, 59
Sawyer, Amos, 118
Schatzberg, Michael, 85
Schlesinger, Arthur, Jr., 6
Schwartzkopf, H. Norman, 99
Sears, Mason, 5–6
Selassie, Haile, II, 77, 78, 79
Select Committee on Intelligence, 63
Senate Foreign Relations Committee, 81, 94
Sewell, John, 60
Seychelles, 22
Sharia, 87
Shultz, George, 94–97, 108–9, 110
Shuman, Michael, 73
Smith, Ian, 38
Somalia, 1, 21, 77–81, 98–101; and the Bush administration, 56; congressional debates on, 37; cost of reconstructing, 111; economic performance of, 78; reductions of aid to, 13; and the Soviet Union, 79; and trade among African nations, 22

South Africa, 4, 21, 23, 101, 106–7, 108–9, 111, 118; American newspapers in, 20; and the Byrd amendment, 38; church leaders in, 106, 116–17, 121; and the Council on African Affairs, 32; and foundations, 74; number of Americans who visited, in 1959, 41; and the Reagan administration, 96, 101, 105–6; sanctions against, 47, 48, 108, 110; statehood of, 21; and the U.S.–South Africa Sister Community Project, 72; and U.S. trade with Africa, 16, 17

Southern Africa, 21, 37. *See also* specific countries

Southern Center for InternationalAffairs, 121

Soviet Union, 6–7, 38, 55–56, 62–63, 76; and Angola, 16, 38; and the arms race, 2; and the Bush administration, 48; and the Carter administration, 44; Cline on, 15; and Cuba, 9; and Ethiopia, 12, 38, 79, 88; and the Horn of Africa, 13, 79; Kissinger on, 10; and Liberia, 92, 93; and Namibia, 12; and the Nixon administration, 9; and the Reagan administration, 49; and South Africa, 104, 106; and Sudan, 83. *See also* Cold War

Stacy, Roy, 96

State Department (U.S.), 4, 7–8, 26, 27; and the black lobby, 32; Bureau of African Affairs, 46; and Liberia, 95

Strange, Susan, 74–75

Sudan, 1, 6, 21, 23, 77–79, 83–89, 90–91, 95; and the Bush administration, 56; church leaders in, 114–17; Communist Party, 83; congressional debates on, 37; economic performance of, 78; reductions of aid to, 13; and trade among African nations, 22

Sullivan, Leon, 34

SuperBowl broadcast (1990), 70

Swaziland, 21

Swing, William, 93, 94

Tabane, Paride, 115

Tambo, Oliver, 106

Tanzania, 22, 23, 24

Tarnoff, Peter, 41

Taylor, Charles, 95, 118

Tigrean People's Liberation Front, 115

Tocqueville, Alexis de, 71

Tolbert, William, 92

TransAfrica, 33–34, 120–23

Truman administration, 5

Tubman, William, 92

Tunisia, 6, 22

Tutu, Desmond, 104–8, 115, 121

UAW (United Automobile Workers), 108

Uganda, 21, 22

UMW (United Mineworkers of America), 108

Ungar, Sanford, 20, 39

UNITA (Uniao Nacional para a Independencia Total de Angola), 9, 12, 47, 52

United Kingdom, 66

United Nations, 42, 67; and the Congo, 80; Non-Governmental Liaison Service, 123; and the Persian Gulf crisis, 56–57; sanctions, 38, 48; Trusteeship Council, 5–6

University of California, 108

USAID (U.S. Agency for International Development), 42, 58, 72, 95, 102

USIA (U.S. Information Agency), 122–25

U.S. News and World Report, 86

U.S.–South Africa Sister Community Project, 72

Vance, Cyrus, 11

Vietnam War, 10, 27, 29, 49, 71

Vosh International, 73

Waltz, Kenneth, 61

Washington Times, 42

Watergate scandal, 49
Wattenberg, Ben, 57, 70
Weh-Sehn, Thomas, 93
West Africa, 22. *See also* specific
 countries
Wilkins, Roy, 32
Williams, G. Mennen, 27, 45–46
Wilson, Woodrow, 58
Wolpe, Howard, 93
Women's World Banking, 73
World Almanac, 71
World Bank, 67, 85, 112
World Neighbors, 72
World Vision, 37, 101,, 107
World War II, 1, 5, 36, 40; attacks
 that led to, 56; "effect," 63;
 Ghana's independence after, 25;
 number of NGOs since, increase
 in, 69–70; post-, internationalist

policies, 62; reconstruction of Europe and Japan after, 111; total
 global product after, 63
World Watch, 70

YMCA, 37, 123
Young, Andrew, 32–33, 42
Young, Crawford, 85

Zaire, 1, 13, 84–87, 95, 98, 100,
 118; church leaders in, 114–17;
 civil war in, 77; congressional
 debates on, 37; economic performance of, 78; and Mobutu, 79–
 85; U.S. assistance to, 28, 37,
 77–81
Zambia, 21, 23, 24
Zimbabwe, 21, 38, 77, 114
Zulu, 23

ABOUT THE AUTHOR

Michael Clough has been the Senior Fellow for Africa at the Council on Foreign Relations since 1987. He served as study director for the Secretary of State's Advisory Committee on Africa in 1986–87. In addition, he has taught at the University of Wisconsin, Madison, and the Naval Postgraduate School. Mr. Clough is a member of the board of Africa Watch and has served as a consultant to CBS News. His articles on U.S. policy toward Africa have appeared in *Foreign Affairs, Foreign Policy,* the *Washington Post,* the *Los Angeles Times,* and other publications.